Best Practice for Experimental Methods in Architecture

Chandler J. Zolan

Best Practice for Experimental Methods in Architecture

A Concise Guide From A/B Testing to Virtual Reality

Springer

Chandler J. Zolan
Texas A&M University
College Station, TX, USA

ISBN 978-3-032-15883-3 ISBN 978-3-032-15884-0 (eBook)
https://doi.org/10.1007/978-3-032-15884-0

This Springer imprint is published by the registered company Springer Nature Switzerland AG
The registered company address is: Gewerbestrasse 11, 6330 Cham, Switzerland

I owe a particular debt of gratitude to Maisie McCormack, whose expertise in experimental design fundamentally informed my understanding of the subject. Her contribution has been indispensable.

Disclosure Statement

The author reports there are no competing interests to declare.

Contents

About the Author

Chandler J. Zolan is a PhD student in the Department of Architecture at Texas A&M University. Coming from a background of security and criminal justice, his research focuses on tacit security measures in pro-social architecture to defend critical infrastructure against natural disasters, criminal, and terroristic behavior. His research investigates causal relationships and examines the role of decision-making within built environments. To achieve this, he conducts a range of experiments, including survey experiments, those integrated with virtual reality, and specialized red-team exercises. The empirical data gleaned from these experiments, especially valuable for illuminating causal relationships, are then leveraged to train machine learning models with the goal of improving security, safety, and quality of life within physical environments.

chandlerzolan.com

Chapter 1
Introduction to Experimental Methods in Architecture

Architecture is where intuition, creativity, and tradition intersect with physics, psychology, and engineering. Yet too often, design decisions are made based on convention, personal preference, or untested assumptions. Empirical research offers a way to move beyond this: it equips architects with a systematic approach to asking questions, gathering evidence, and drawing conclusions that can be tested, repeated, and trusted. It provides the foundation for a discipline that aspires not just to inspire, but also to perform.

Before discussing experimental methods in detail, it is necessary to clarify what is—and is not—meant by "experiment" in the context of architectural research. Architectural studies are often broadly referred to as "empirical" when they involve data collection or observation. However, not all empirical research is experimental. Empirical methods include a wide range of approaches—such as case studies, surveys, ethnographies, post-occupancy evaluations, and observational research—that aim to gather knowledge from experience or measurement. What distinguishes experimental methods is their ability to identify causal relationships through systematic intervention and control.

Mastering experimental methods is not merely an academic exercise; it is a critical skill set with profound implications for both emerging scholars and established practitioners in architecture. A robust understanding of experimental methodologies is indispensable for conducting rigorous research. It provides the framework for formulating testable hypotheses, designing robust studies, collecting credible data, and drawing defensible conclusions. These methods also serve to elevate architectural practice from reliance on intuition and convention to a truly evidence-based design paradigm. By systematically testing design interventions and evaluating their outcomes, architects can create better-performing buildings that optimize for human experience, environmental sustainability, and functional efficiency. This approach leads to more defensible design decisions, grounded in empirical data rather than subjective preference, which can also translate into new professional

C. J. Zolan, *Best Practice for Experimental Methods in Architecture*,
https://doi.org/10.1007/978-3-032-15884-0_1

opportunities and expanded advisory roles, such as specialized consulting on building performance, post-occupancy evaluations, or strategic design optimization.

While the broad umbrella of "empirical research" encompasses any systematic inquiry based on observed or measured phenomena, it is imperative for rigorous architectural scholarship to differentiate clearly between general empirical approaches and true experimental methods. This distinction is not merely semantic; it carries profound implications for the nature of the claims that can be made and the conclusions that can be drawn from a study. Empirical research broadly refers to any investigation that gathers evidence through direct or indirect observation or experience. This includes a wide spectrum of methodologies such as case studies, observational studies, ethnographies, qualitative interviews, and various forms of surveys, all of which are invaluable for describing phenomena, exploring relationships, or understanding contexts. However, the hallmark of a true experiment, as defined within the scientific method, is its unique capacity to establish causal relationships. An experiment is characterized by three core elements:

1. *Manipulation of an Independent Variable*: The researcher actively intervenes by controlling and changing one or more independent variables within the study environment.
2. *Random Assignment*: Participants or units of analysis are randomly assigned to different experimental conditions.
3. *Control of Extraneous Variables*: Efforts are made to minimize other factors that could influence the outcome, thereby isolating the effect of the independent variable on the dependent variable.

To achieve the deliberate manipulation of one or more independent variables and holding other factors constant, experiments require a controlled environment, random assignment to conditions, and—where possible—blinding, in order to minimize bias. For example, if one wishes to know whether the color of a classroom influences concentration, a true experiment would require assigning participants randomly to rooms of different colors, ensuring all other factors (e.g. lighting, temperature, noise) remain constant, and then measuring task performance. In practice, architecture rarely affords such clean conditions. Full control over environmental variables is difficult or impossible outside laboratory settings, and ethical constraints often prevent random assignment in real-world spaces. As a result, much of architectural experimentation falls into the category of quasi-experiments—research that lacks full randomization or control but still seeks to infer causal relationships by manipulating conditions in structured ways. Examples include testing two different wayfinding systems in similar hospital wings, or introducing a design intervention in a public plaza and measuring behavioral changes before and after. However, true experimentation can be achieved through simulation environments, mock-ups, immersive digital models, and controlled spatial prototypes. They all offer ways to test hypotheses while approximating ecological validity.

Without random assignment, a study, however empirical, remains correlational. While correlations can suggest relationships and generate hypotheses, they cannot definitively prove that one variable causes another. True experiments, by virtue of their design, aim to approximate the "counterfactual"—what would have happened to the same units had they *not* received the treatment—by comparing randomly assigned groups. This meticulous control is what empowers experiments to move beyond mere observation to assertive claims of causality, forming the bedrock of evidence-based advancements in any discipline, including architecture.

A particularly flexible tool for architectural researchers is the survey experiment. These combine the broad reach of survey methods with the logic of experimental design. In a survey experiment, different participants are shown different visual, textual, or spatial stimuli—such as alternate renderings of a design or varying spatial descriptions—and are then asked to respond. Because the variation in stimuli is controlled, and the outcomes are measured quantitatively, survey experiments can isolate the effects of specific design features on perception, preference, or decision-making. This approach is particularly useful when testing human responses to architecture before construction, and it is one of the most adaptable and accessible forms of experimentation available to design researchers today. Ultimately, the goal of experimentation in architecture is not to recreate the clinical purity of laboratory science, but to bring rigor, transparency, and causal reasoning into design research. Experimental thinking enables architects to move beyond correlation and toward explanation—making their insights more transferable, their designs more justifiable, and their process more robust.

Empirical methods—especially those implemented before construction—offer a crucial opportunity: the chance to evaluate the impact of a design before it becomes physically embedded in the built environment. This a priori experimentation enables architects to refine their work iteratively, improving outcomes for users, clients, and communities without relying on post-occupancy hindsight. Design mock-ups, simulations, physical and digital prototypes, and controlled environment testing all serve as ways to predict and measure human responses to space—lighting, scale, acoustics, spatial organization—before the first brick is laid or beam is poured. While observational studies can reveal correlations between architectural features and outcomes, experiments allow researchers to manipulate variables and isolate their impact, providing clear evidence of cause-and-effect relationships. For example, does the introduction of natural materials in a school setting actually reduce stress and increase concentration, or does it merely correlate with better funding and location? Do wider corridors in hospitals measurably improve wayfinding and reduce staff fatigue, or is the relationship more nuanced? Only controlled, replicable studies—true experiments—can answer such questions with the clarity and confidence the profession increasingly demands.

Architecture is entering a new phase of accountability. As expectations for sustainability, accessibility, and performance increase, so too does the need for design decisions backed by more than tradition or taste. Experimental methods enable architects to respond to that challenge. They allow us to ask not just "what looks good" or "what feels right," but "what works best?" And most importantly: "how do we know?" Understanding what works in architecture is only part of the picture; knowing why it works, how it works, and under what conditions it works is what gives that knowledge real power. Architects rarely design in controlled vacuums—site conditions, user needs, cultural expectations, and environmental constraints vary dramatically. Without understanding the mechanisms that drive outcomes, design decisions risk being contextually fragile or misunderstood when replicated. Knowing that daylight improves concentration, for instance, is less useful than understanding how it influences neurological alertness, why it matters at certain times of day, or what thresholds make it effective. Mechanistic understanding not only strengthens generalizability, but also supports cross-cultural applicability and iterative refinement—enabling architects to adapt findings across contexts, refine interventions over time, and build a cumulative, transferable knowledge base. For a field that must increasingly demonstrate measurable impact—on well-being, performance, and sustainability—understanding the "why" behind a design outcome is not just intellectually satisfying, it's essential for credibility, accountability, and innovation.

The timing of experimentation also matters. Conducting research a priori—before construction takes place—offers distinct and often underutilized advantages. First and most obviously, it mitigates cost. Testing ideas through simulation, prototypes, or controlled interventions allows designers to identify inefficiencies, design flaws, or poor user outcomes without committing to expensive materials, labor, or rework. Second, it accelerates learning. Architects can explore multiple hypotheses quickly and isolate causal relationships in ways that would be infeasible post-occupancy. Third, a priori research expands design freedom: when architects understand probable outcomes in advance, they can make bolder, better-informed decisions with reduced uncertainty. Finally, early-stage experimentation helps secure stakeholder buy-in—clients, funders, and planning bodies are more likely to support innovative or high-cost interventions when presented with empirical evidence predicting success. In short, empirical work before construction maximizes the efficiency, accountability, and adaptability of architectural practice, while reducing the risks typically associated with design speculation.

By embracing empirical experimentation, architects become better equipped to design buildings that are not just beautiful, but truly effective—spaces that support well-being, enable productivity, and adapt to the complex realities of human life. In fields such as aerospace, product design, and medicine, a priori testing is a well-established standard; prototypes are rigorously evaluated, simulations run, and interventions refined before costly production or deployment. Compared to these disciplines, architecture has traditionally been slower to adopt a systematic, experimental mindset prior to construction, often relying on precedent, intuition, or post-occupancy evaluations. This lag carries significant risks such as costly design errors, missed opportunities for innovation, and sometimes, negative impacts on occupant health and safety. Integrating empirical experimentation early in the design process transforms architecture from a speculative art into a responsible, evidence-driven practice. In this way, experiments in architecture are not just scientific exercises; they are deliberate acts of responsibility, creativity, and care.

This book builds a comprehensive foundation for designing and conducting rigorous experimental research in architecture, with a particular focus on survey-based methods that address the field's current challenges and future opportunities. The opening chapter defines key experimental concepts and distinguishes between experimental, quasi-experimental, and observational approaches. Practical chapters then guide readers through core experimental designs—including A/B testing, factorial designs, and within- and between-subjects methods—equipping researchers with tools to manage variables and interpret complex data. Further sections explore advanced topics such as robustness checks, pilot testing, and ethical considerations, ensuring research is both reliable and responsible. The book also highlights cutting-edge techniques like virtual reality simulations, demonstrating how emerging technologies can enhance experimental control and realism. Finally, the conclusion addresses broader issues of external validity, effective communication of results, and the evolving future of architectural experimentation, including the integration of artificial intelligence and new data analysis methods. Together, these chapters aim to empower architects, researchers, and students to move beyond intuition toward evidence-based, user-centered, and innovative design practice.

Chapter 2
What Are Experimental Methods?

Chapter Definitions

Independent Variable (IV, denoted as X)

The factor that the researcher deliberately manipulates in an experiment. It is the theorized "cause" in a cause-and-effect relationship. The experimenter changes X to observe its effect on another variable.

Example: Varying the transparency levels of a facade material (20% vs 50% vs 80% visible light transmittance) to assess impact of light on perceived privacy in an office.

Dependent Variable (DV, denoted as Y)

The outcome that is observed. It is the presumed "effect" in a cause-and-effect relationship, and its value is hypothesized to depend on the changes made to the independent variable.

Example: User ratings of privacy levels within different light transmittance into an office space.

While the term might conjure an image of scientists and test tubes, the experiments we can use in architecture will ordinarily look quite different. An experiment is simply a systematic research method used to establish causal relationships between variables by deliberately manipulating one or more independent variables and measuring their effects on dependent variables. Unlike observational studies, which only identify correlations, experiments involve direct intervention to isolate the influence of specific factors while controlling for external influences.

Experiments in architectural research are inherently iterative, serving as a vital tool for refining design concepts ideally before construction begins. By systematically testing hypotheses and gathering feedback in controlled settings, architects can identify unforeseen issues, validate assumptions, and optimize design elements. This iterative process bridges theory and practice, allowing for informed adjustments that enhance the final built environment's effectiveness and user experience. Through repeated cycles of experimentation and refinement, designs evolve in

C. J. Zolan, *Best Practice for Experimental Methods in Architecture*,
https://doi.org/10.1007/978-3-032-15884-0_2

response to empirical evidence rather than intuition alone, reducing uncertainty and improving confidence in architectural decisions.

Experimental approaches in architecture have roots in early behavioral design pioneers who sought to understand how people interact with spaces. Christopher Alexander's *Pattern Language* (1977) marked a significant step by proposing repeatable design "patterns" grounded in observed human needs and behaviors. Similarly, studies from the 1960s began systematically examining institutional and public buildings to inform better spatial layouts and user experiences. The Bauhaus and broader Modernist movements also emphasized rationality, functionality, and scientific principles in design, challenging traditional aesthetics and intuition-driven methods. However, despite these early advances, the field largely remained reliant on precedent, personal authority, and stylistic conventions, often without rigorous testing or systematic validation. In recent decades, however, there has been a notable shift toward "evidence-based design"—particularly in sectors such as healthcare and education—where observational methods have been embraced to improve outcomes like patient recovery rates and student performance. This shift represents a turning point for architecture, moving it closer to a research-informed discipline where design decisions are supported by empirical data rather than solely by tradition or expert opinion.

The iconic Eames House (Case Study House #8), designed by Charles and Ray Eames and completed in 1949, represents one of the most famous architectural experiments in history. Designed to test the practical application of post-war prefabricated materials, modular construction, and the seamless integration of art and life, the building served as a "living laboratory" for over five decades. The Eameses continuously tested and documented everything from the performance of their off-the-shelf steel components to the optimal placement of furniture under shifting daylight angles. While this highly personal, longitudinal approach generated invaluable qualitative insights into flexible living and sustainable design principles, it fundamentally remained a single-case study. Today, by contrast, the need for rigorous experimental tools is paramount. The Eames House model lacks the control and statistical power necessary to make causal claims; it could not isolate the effect of the steel frame from the effect of the Eameses themselves. By developing methodologies like between-subjects designs and high-fidelity VR modeling, we move beyond mere documentation and observation to establish causal relationships—allowing us to prove why a particular design choice works, rather than simply showing that it did for one extraordinary couple.

If the Eames House was a "living lab" of observation, Cedric Price's unbuilt Fun Palace (1960s) was a massive conceptual experiment, framing architecture not as a static object, but as a responsive, adaptable system. Price envisioned the Fun Palace as a highly flexible environment controlled by automated cranes, movable walls, and modular components, where the design was constantly reconfigured by user need and whim. Though never fully realized, Price's team utilized theoretical simulations and small-scale prototypes to test the project's extreme adaptability and user-driven programming—an early, analog form of systems modeling. This work fundamentally influenced concepts of flexible architecture and participatory design, positioning the structure as a reactive device rather than a dictatorial container. Today, we achieve Price's core experimental goals with tools he couldn't imagine: where Price used theory and drawing to model systemic adaptability, architects now employ VR, parametric modeling, and Agent-Based Modeling (ABM) to digitally simulate thousands of user-defined variables and test the causal impact of flexibility before a single piece of steel is ordered. This transition from conceptual prototypes to validated digital simulation is where the experimental method finds its modern power, demanding a methodology that can finally deliver on the promise of evidence-based design.

This growing reliance on data has laid the groundwork for more rigorous empirical methodologies—especially experimental approaches that go beyond correlation to identify causality. As architecture increasingly seeks to validate the effectiveness of design decisions, experiments are essential tools for isolating and testing the specific mechanisms that drive user experience and behavioral outcomes. An experiment is designed to establish causal relationships between variables by systematically manipulating one or more independent variables and observing their effect on one or more dependent variables while keeping all else equal. Mathematically, an experiment follows this structure:

$$Y = f\left(X, \epsilon\right)$$

where

- Y = dependent variable (e.g., perceived spaciousness of a room).
- X = independent variable(s) (e.g., ceiling height, lighting conditions).
- ϵ = Error term, representing unexplained variance.

The goal of an experiment is to isolate the effect of X on Y by random assignment, ensuring that ϵ is minimized.

Causality in an experiment is established by actively changing the independent variable while keeping all other factors constant (Imai et al., 2011). This ensures that any observed differences in the dependent variable are directly caused by the manipulation and not by external influences. For an experiment to be truly causal, the researcher must have full control over the independent variable. Consider an experiment examining how ceiling height affects people's perception of spaciousness in a room. In this case, ceiling height is the independent variable. To test its effect, we create several versions of the same room, ensuring that everything remains identical except for the ceiling height, which might vary between 8 ft, 10 ft, and 12 ft. Each participant experiences only one version of the room, and they are randomly assigned to a condition. This random assignment eliminates selection bias by ensuring that individual differences, such as personal preferences or previous experiences, do not systematically influence the results. By holding all other variables constant—such as lighting, wall color, and furniture layout—we ensure that the only difference between groups is the ceiling height itself.

For a real-world application, consider the problem of patient room materiality. An architecture firm, collaborating with a research team, may hypothesize that the presence of biophilic wood grain textures (X_1) and a direct outdoor view (X_2) reduce patient anxiety (Y). They could build a high-fidelity mock-up of a standard patient room and randomly assign groups of participants (patients, staff, and visitors) to experience one of four conditions: laminate wood grain/no view, laminate wood grain/outdoor view, painted drywall/no view, or painted drywall/outdoor view. By systematically isolating the effects of the specific surface material and the access to nature, and measuring physiological stress markers (the dependent variable, Y), the team moves beyond mere correlation. They can then definitively state: "It's the access to the outdoor view, not the wood texture, that causally reduces anxiety in this specific environment."

A Note on Notations

X, X_1, X_2.... where does it all end?

In mathematical notation, we assign letters to represent variables we are studying. This could be 'number of stories', and that would be X. When a variable says X_1, we are referring to the first observation of that in our design. So, for example, a building design may be tested as X_1 and X_2 which would correspond to whether the building has Design A (3 stories) or Design B (4 stories).

You might consider... why not X_3 and X_4 then? It is important to remember that the subscript simply indexes the observation–it does not indicate the value of the variable itself.

It is this isolation of the independent variable which allows us to confidently attribute any changes in perceived spaciousness to the ceiling height rather than to other environmental factors. If these conditions are met, we can express the causal effect using the potential outcomes framework, which defines the causal effect of an independent variable by comparing two potential outcomes:

$$\text{Causal Effect} = Y(1) - Y(0)$$

where

- $Y(1)$ = outcome when exposed to treatment (e.g., a certain design feature)
- $Y(0)$ = outcome when not exposed (control condition)

This formulation, rooted in Rubin's causal model, ensures that any observed difference is truly caused by X rather than external influences, which are captured by the error term ϵ. However, in reality, we can never observe both $Y(1)$ and $Y(0)$ for the same individual—this is known as the fundamental problem of causal inference. Instead, we rely on experimental design techniques such as randomization to approximate this comparison at a group level, ensuring that differences between groups are due to X and not pre-existing biases or confounding variables.

ϵ

ϵ (the error term) represents everything that affects the dependent variable (Y) that is not explained by the independent variable (X).

In a well-designed experiment, ϵ would include unmeasured factors such as participants' prior experiences, mood, background noise, or even subconscious biases–essentially, any external influence or random variation not controlled for in the experiment.

By using random assignment and holding other variables constant, the goal is to reduce the influence of these uncontrolled factors, thereby minimizing ϵ and isolating the true causal effect of X on Y.

Random assignment is a fundamental principle of experimental design that ensures groups are comparable before the manipulation of the independent variable (Kirk, 2009). By randomly allocating participants to different experimental conditions, researchers prevent systematic differences between groups that could otherwise distort the causal relationship being studied. This process equalizes the distribution of potential confounding variables, such as individual preferences, prior experiences, or demographic factors, reducing the likelihood that these extraneous factors influence the results. This may seem counterintuitive at first. Those unfamiliar with experimental design often focus on the demographic composition of the groups, assuming that balance must be ensured manually. As a result, researchers commonly collect demographic data to address these concerns—even though, in a properly randomized experiment, such balance is expected by design. Ironically, the practice of highlighting demographic comparisons can reinforce the misconception that randomization is insufficient on its own.

Conceptualizing Randomization

Imagine dealing hands from a well-shuffled deck of cards. The larger each hand, the more closely it will reflect the overall composition of the deck–roughly equal numbers of suits and ranks. Similarly, in an experiment, larger groups assigned at random are more likely to balance participant characteristics (like demographics) across conditions. This balance arises naturally through chance, reinforcing why random assignment works best with sufficiently large sample sizes.

In a randomized experiment, individual characteristics—such as age, sex, or background—are distributed randomly across conditions. This means that, on average, the groups will be statistically equivalent with respect to both measured and unmeasured traits. The purpose of random assignment is precisely to avoid the need for manual balancing. If randomization is properly implemented and sample sizes are sufficient, demographic comparability is achieved by design. The collection of demographic data ought to be done not to balance groups post hoc, but only to verify that randomization worked as expected and to test whether any observed effects differ across subgroups. If major imbalances appear despite randomization, experimentalists conduct robustness checks or re-run the randomization process, but this is rarely necessary with reasonable sample sizes.

Imagine a firm is testing the optimal layout for a new university library's study space: a traditional, desk-focused layout (Condition A) versus a more social, collaborative pod system (Condition B). If the researchers *didn't* use random assignment—say, if students who already prefer collaborative work tend to naturally choose Condition B—then any observed increase in "perceived productivity" (Y) in Condition B would be hopelessly confounded with pre-existing preference (Z). Randomization is the necessary blunt instrument. It doesn't care if 70% of participants are engineering majors; it just ensures that, on average, the engineers, the literature students, and the late-night coffee addicts are equally distributed across both the traditional and the pod system groups. The causal effect is therefore isolated from all those pesky, pre-existing individual differences.

One of the primary benefits of randomization is its ability to eliminate selection bias (Casler, 2015). In non-randomized studies, participants might self-select into conditions based on underlying characteristics, making it difficult to determine whether observed differences in the dependent variable are caused by the independent variable or by pre-existing differences between participants. Randomization disrupts this possibility by ensuring that each participant has an equal chance of being assigned to any condition, creating groups that are statistically similar before the experiment begins. As a result, any differences observed after the manipulation can more confidently be attributed to the independent variable rather than external factors.

That is not to say that randomization eliminates all threats to validity. Unobserved confounders—variables that influence both the independent and dependent variables but are not accounted for in the study—may still pose a risk, particularly with small sample sizes. Non-random attrition, where participants drop out of different conditions at unequal rates, can also introduce bias if the remaining participants are no longer representative of the original groups (Mitchell et al., 2022). To mitigate these risks, researchers must carefully design their studies: ensuring sufficient sample sizes, monitoring attrition, and conducting robustness checks to confirm that randomization has effectively balanced potential confounders. In this context, control variables also play a critical role. In experiments, "control variables" refer to all aspects of the setting that are deliberately held constant across all groups—made possible by the researcher's direct control over the experimental setup. This is a major advantage over observational methods, where statistical adjustments must be made post hoc to account for confounding differences. Physical control in experiments allows researchers to reduce bias at the design stage, reinforcing internal validity and enabling more confident causal claims.

In practice, experimental designs in architecture often rely on surveys to capture participants' reactions and perceptions of different conditions. These conditions could involve exposure to a variety of architectural stimuli such as photographs of spaces, written descriptions, or even virtual walkthroughs that simulate real-world environments. By controlling for these external variables, researchers can isolate specific factors of interest, such as lighting, spatial layout, or material textures and evaluate their impact on the dependent variables. Once participants have been exposed to these stimuli, a series of carefully designed questions are posed to assess the dependent variables, which may include measures of comfort, mood, spatial perception, or satisfaction with the space. These questions should be aligned with the theoretical constructs being studied, ensuring that the questions are directly related to the experimental design and will capture meaningful data that can support or refute the research hypothesis. This approach—where participants are randomly assigned to different visual or textual stimuli and then asked to report their reactions—forms the basis of survey experiments, which are especially useful in architectural research for isolating subjective impressions, preferences, or perceived effects. These will be explored in detail in later chapters.

While true experiments, with their hallmark of random assignment, are certainly the gold standard for establishing causal inference, architectural research may confront scenarios where such rigorous control is simply not feasible or ethical. In these instances, quasi-experiments and natural experiments can tempt as alternatives.

However, it is important to be aware of their inherent limitations. Quasi-experiments are research designs that superficially resemble true experiments, but critically, they lack random assignment to treatment and control groups. Instead, they rely on pre-existing groups or naturally occurring variations in an independent variable. For example, comparing the energy consumption of two existing buildings, one with a novel facade system and one with a conventional one, or evaluating the impact of a new urban planning policy by comparing areas where it was implemented versus areas where it was not, exemplify quasi-experimental approaches. Similarly, natural experiments capitalize on naturally occurring events or policy changes that effectively create "treatment" and "control" conditions without any researcher intervention. Observing how a city's street life changes after a major pedestrianization project, or comparing the thermal comfort in homes built before and after a new insulation code, are examples. Here, the "experiment" is conducted by nature or policy, and the researcher's role is to meticulously observe and analyze the consequences.

It is paramount to recognize, however, that despite the inclusion of "experiment" in their names, these designs are fundamentally observational studies. Their core limitation lies in their inability to definitively establish causality with the same certainty as a true randomized experiment. Because participants or units are not randomly assigned, there is always the critical risk of unobserved confounding variables—factors that differ between the groups and influence the outcome, but are not accounted for in the study. These pre-existing differences can easily obscure or distort the true effect of the intervention, making it unreliable to confidently assert that an observed outcome was caused by the architectural design or policy change, rather than by some other, unmeasured, covarying factor. By lending them the term "experiment" at all, there is a distinct risk of tempting casual readers or less methodologically discerning individuals into perceiving the results as more robust and causally conclusive than they actually are. This misrepresentation undermines the pursuit of rigorous evidence and should be actively discouraged.

Therefore, while acknowledging their practical necessity for identifying associations or exploring phenomena in complex, real-world architectural contexts, it is crucial to recognize that these designs are intrinsically insufficient for proving direct causation. A more scientifically robust path, when feasible, involves thinking creatively about how to recreate or simulate environments with controlled conditions. This might involve high-fidelity virtual reality simulations, meticulously constructed mock-ups, or controlled spatial prototypes where independent variables can be systematically manipulated and random assignment can be employed. Such approaches, though potentially resource-intensive, offer the methodological precision necessary to isolate causal effects, thereby providing more actionable and generalizable insights for architectural theory and practice.

Where, exactly, does this kind of rigor land in the fast-paced world of architectural practice? The reality is that true experiments rarely occur on a live construction site—that's just too expensive and too late. Instead, the application of experimental methods in architecture is growing through three primary, overlapping channels:

1. In-House R&D Units
   Larger, progressive firms are establishing dedicated research arms or "performance teams." They treat design options like hypotheses, often employing A/B testing or survey experiments (as described below) using digital models, VR simulations, or small-scale mock-ups. Their goal is to generate proprietary data that gives them a competitive edge by demonstrably improving client outcomes (e.g., a workplace design that measurably improves team cohesion). These units were initiated via federal defense contracts who wanted causality-driven design through specialized and often unpublicized working groups, but as this yielded results, these groups have expanded.
2. Academic-Practice Partnerships
   This is often the most fruitful space for fundamental causal research. Firms partner with universities to leverage their methodological expertise, ethics review boards, and access to sophisticated tools (such as physiological measurement equipment). The architect provides the real-world problem and design artifact, and the academic team ensures the rigor of the experimental design. This collaboration allows for high-quality, generalizable research without the firm needing to become a fully fledged research institution itself.
3. Consultant-Driven Evidence-Based Design (EBD)
   Specialized EBD consultants use experimental and quasi-experimental methods to inform early-stage design decisions, particularly in high-stakes sectors like healthcare and education. While much of their work is observational, the drive toward testing specific design interventions—such as the impact of a new patient room layout on nurse workflow—often necessitates small-scale, randomized trials in prototype or simulation spaces. This integration signals a shift toward research being a non-negotiable component of a design contract, not just a post-occupancy nice-to-have.

While architects don't necessarily have to become full-time statisticians, they must become smart consumers and ethical participants in the experimental process, knowing what evidence is *truly* causal and how to ask researchable questions that move the profession forward. Experimental methods provide the most rigorous tools available for testing cause-and-effect relationships in architecture. By systematically manipulating independent variables, randomly assigning participants to conditions, and controlling for external influences, these approaches allow researchers to move beyond intuition and correlation to uncover the mechanisms that truly drive human responses to space. For a field increasingly expected to demonstrate measurable impact—on well-being, performance, sustainability—this shift toward experimental thinking is both timely and essential. Three experimental frameworks stand out as particularly useful for architectural research: A/B testing, factorial design, and within-subjects design. Each offers distinct advantages depending on the research question, practical constraints, and variables under investigation. The following chapters will examine the theoretical foundations of these frameworks, provide practical guidance for implementation, and show how they can be adapted to real-world architectural challenges.

References

Casler, Michael D. "Fundamentals of experimental design: Guidelines for designing successful experiments." *Agronomy Journal* 107, no. 2 (2015): 692–705.

Alexander, Christopher. A pattern language: towns, buildings, construction. Oxford University Press, 1977.

Imai, Kosuke, Luke Keele, Dustin Tingley, and Teppei Yamamoto. "Unpacking the black box of causality: Learning about causal mechanisms from experimental and observational studies." *American Political Science Review* 105, no. 4 (2011): 765–789.

Kirk, Roger E. "Experimental design." *Sage handbook of quantitative methods in psychology* (2009): 23–45.

Mitchell, Meghan M., Chantal Fahmy, Kendra J. Clark, and David C. Pyrooz. "Non-random study attrition: Assessing correction techniques and the magnitude of bias in a longitudinal study of reentry from prison." *Journal of Quantitative Criminology* 38, no. 3 (2022): 755–790.

Chapter 3
A/B Testing: A Practical Guide

Chapter Definitions

External Validity

The extent to which the findings of a study can be applied to other situations, people, or settings beyond the specific context of the experiment.

Example: Did the new, open-plan office layout truly increase employee collaboration, or was it the new collaborative software introduced simultaneously that caused the change?

Internal Validity

The extent to which a study establishes a trustworthy cause-and-effect relationship between the independent and dependent variables, meaning the observed effect is truly due to the intervention and not other factors.

Example: Would placing the same automatic door design at a different office building generate the same improvements in perceived accessibility?

Having established the foundational principles of experimental methods and distinguished true experiments from observational studies, we now turn to one of the most direct, simplistic, and widely applicable forms of randomized control experimentation: A/B testing. Often perceived as a tool primarily for digital interfaces, A/B testing, at its core, embodies the systematic rigor of experimental design, making it an extraordinarily powerful approach for architectural research and practice. It allows designers and researchers to move beyond intuition, testing specific interventions with a precision that yields clear, actionable insights into what truly works and why.

In an A/B test, two or more versions of a design—referred to as "A" (the control) and "B" (the experimental condition)—are tested with different groups of participants, allowing for direct comparison of their effects. For example, an architect might use A/B testing to compare two different lighting schemes in a room, with one group exposed to one scheme (A) and another group exposed to the other (B).

C. J. Zolan, *Best Practice for Experimental Methods in Architecture*,
https://doi.org/10.1007/978-3-032-15884-0_3

By randomizing which participants are exposed to each condition, A/B testing eliminates bias and helps establish causality, showing whether one design choice has a significant advantage over another. This method enables architects to make data-driven decisions, identifying the most effective design elements based on measurable outcomes, such as user satisfaction, behavior, or environmental performance. A/B testing can be especially useful in refining designs, testing new ideas in real-world contexts, and ensuring that architectural decisions are optimized for the needs of the people who will use the space.

The mathematical framework used in A/B testing is based on comparing the means or distributions of outcomes between two groups, often using hypothesis testing and statistical analysis to determine whether observed differences are significant. At the core of A/B testing, we assume that there are two conditions:

1. A (Control group): The baseline or standard design condition.
2. B (Treatment group): The experimental condition where the design is altered in some way.

The key concept is that by randomly assigning participants to one of the two conditions, we control for any confounding variables, ensuring that the only difference between the groups is the design feature being tested (Kohavi and Longbotham, 2015). Mathematically, the outcome of interest for each participant is denoted as Y. In a typical A/B test, we are interested in the average treatment effect (ATE), which is defined as:

$$\text{ATE} = E\left[Y(1)\right] - E\left[Y(0)\right]$$

where

- $Y(1)$ is the outcome when the participant is exposed to the treatment (design feature B).
- $Y(0)$ is the outcome when the participant is exposed to the control (design feature A).
- $E[]$ denotes the expected value (or mean) of the outcomes for each group.

To test whether the difference between A and B is statistically significant, we calculate the difference in means (or other appropriate test statistic) between the two groups. This is usually done using a *t*-test (for continuous outcomes, Appendix I) or a chi-square test (for categorical outcomes, Appendix II). The null hypothesis (H_0) typically states that there is no difference between A and B, and the alternative hypothesis (H_A) states that a difference does exist.

$$H_0 : E\left[Y(1)\right] = E\left[Y(0)\right]$$

$$H_A : E\left[Y(1)\right] \neq E\left[Y(0)\right]$$

If the test statistic indicates that the difference is statistically significant (i.e., the p-value is less than the chosen significance level, often 0.05), we reject the null hypothesis and conclude that the change in design (from A to B) led to a meaningful difference in outcomes. The power of the A/B test (typically set at 0.9 or 90%) ensures that there is a 90% chance of detecting a true effect, if it exists, and helps determine the appropriate sample size needed to achieve reliable results. If there is no significant difference, it suggests that the change may not have had the expected effect. However, it is important to remember that a lack of significance does not prove that there is no effect—it simply means the data do not support a strong effect based on the sample size and conditions tested. To build confidence in the results, it's helpful to replicate the A/B test in different settings, with different participants, or at different times. This helps verify whether the design change consistently yields the same results. Through randomization and the control of confounding variables, A/B testing allows researchers to establish causality, meaning that any observed differences in the outcome can be attributed to the specific design change, rather than to other external factors (Kohavi et al., 2020). This makes A/B testing a powerful tool for making evidence-based decisions in architecture and design.

Power analysis is crucial in A/B testing experiments to ensure that the test is designed to detect a meaningful difference between versions A and B, if one exists. It helps determine the appropriate sample size needed to achieve reliable results. The goal of power analysis is to avoid wasting resources on tests that are too small to produce trustworthy conclusions, while also ensuring that the sample size isn't unnecessarily large, which can be costly and time-consuming (Steidl and Thomas, 2001). The essence of power analysis lies in understanding statistical power, which is the probability of correctly rejecting the null hypothesis when there is a true difference between the two versions. Typically, the desired statistical power is 80%, meaning there's an 80% chance of detecting an effect if it truly exists. When conducting an A/B test, power analysis helps you calculate the sample size needed to achieve this power, ensuring that the test is sufficiently sensitive to identify meaningful effects.

The sample size required for an A/B test is influenced by several factors: the expected effect size, which represents the smallest meaningful difference between the two groups that you wish to detect, the alpha level (significance level), typically set at 0.05, which represents the threshold for deciding whether to reject the null hypothesis, and the variance or standard deviation within the groups. Larger sample sizes are needed when the effect size is small, or when the data is more variable. Without power analysis, there's a risk of conducting a test with an insufficient sample size, which could lead to Type II errors (false negatives), where you fail to detect a difference that actually exists.

Conceptualizing Type II Errors

In a game of poker, your opponent makes smaller bets when they have a strong hand, to lull you into calling. However, you instead call every time they take a sip of their drink during their turn because you are paying attention to conventional tells. Consequently, you repeatedly fail to detect this consistent, strategic betting pattern, and you continue to believe their bet sizing is just standard or arbitrary (failing to reject the null hypothesis that their bet sizing is random). This failure to identify their actual, consistent strategy, even though it's actively influencing the game, is a Type II error: a real, underlying effect (the opponent's deliberate strategy) was at play, but your "analysis" (your observation and interpretation) was not sensitive or comprehensive enough to detect it, leading you to a false negative conclusion about their play.

Conversely, a test with a sample size that's too large may not only be wasteful but could also increase the time and resources required to complete the experiment. Various software tools and online calculators can help with this process, including *R* and *GPower*, which use the following basis:

$$\text{Sample Size} = \left(Z\alpha/2 + Z\beta\right)^2 * \left(2 * \sigma^2\right) / \left(d^2\right)$$

where

- $Z\alpha/2$ is the Z-value corresponding to the alpha level (for 0.05, it's 1.96)
- $Z\beta$ is the Z-value corresponding to the desired power level (for 90% power, it's 1.28)
- σ is the standard deviation of the groups
- d is the effect size (the difference you want to detect)

A/B testing can take various forms depending on the research objectives, design, and data being collected. One common type is the basic A/B test, where two variations of a treatment, design, or product are compared directly to measure their impact on a specific outcome. This could involve testing different website layouts to see which results in higher user engagement or testing two marketing messages to determine which drives more conversions. Another variation is a multi-armed bandit test, which is similar to an A/B test but dynamically adjusts the distribution of traffic between the different variants based on performance during the experiment (Xiang et al., 2022). This can optimize for the best performing variant more quickly. There are also split URL tests, where the two versions of a webpage are hosted on different URLs rather than just differing elements on the same page (Astachova et al., 2020). This type of test is often used when the changes are more drastic, such as completely different landing pages or user flows. In addition, some A/B tests involve more than two groups, allowing researchers to compare multiple variations simultaneously, providing more information about the relative effectiveness of different treatments. The specific design and type of A/B test chosen depend on the research objectives, the level of confidence needed in the results, and the practical considerations of the experiment. Each type of A/B test requires careful consideration of statistical assumptions and sample size to ensure reliable and valid results.

While A/B testing can provide valuable insights, there are several limitations and potential pitfalls that architecture researchers should be aware of. It is critical to ensure random assignment into A/B condition. If participants are not randomly assigned to the A or B group, or if external factors influence who gets exposed to which variation, the results can be skewed and not reflective of the broader population. Additionally, A/B tests are typically designed to measure a specific outcome or variable, but they may miss broader, more nuanced effects. For example, a test might show that one variant leads to higher conversions, but it may not capture longer-term impacts such as customer satisfaction or retention. Timing is also a crucial consideration. The duration of an A/B test needs to be long enough to account for daily, weekly, or seasonal variations in behavior, but not so long that external factors, such as changes in market conditions or competitor behavior, start influencing the results. A/B tests are often used in highly dynamic environments, and changes made during the test—like design updates or shifts in marketing strategy—can introduce confounding variables that affect the outcome. Another pitfall is assuming causality from correlation. Just because two variations differ in performance, it doesn't necessarily mean one caused the difference; external variables or unaccounted factors could be at play. Finally, while A/B testing is useful for evaluating specific changes, it is not a substitute for a broader, more holistic understanding of human behavior or the overall impact of a product or service. It focuses on short-term outcomes and may not reflect long-term effects or broader trends that are important for strategic decision-making.

While A/B testing in digital realms often emphasizes rapid iteration and short-term outcome measurement, applying this methodology to architectural interventions necessitates a more nuanced consideration of test duration and the nature of the effects being observed. Unlike fleeting online interactions, architectural impacts frequently manifest over protracted periods and involve complex, evolving human-environment dynamics. When designing an A/B test for a built environment, the duration of the study must be carefully calibrated to capture the full spectrum of relevant data. For instance, evaluating the true impact of a facade design on building comfort demands a test period that extends beyond a few days or weeks; it must encompass seasonal variations to account for different solar angles, temperatures, and daylight availability across a full year. Similarly, assessing occupant well-being or productivity linked to a new interior layout cannot rely solely on immediate reactions. Human occupants undergo occupant adaptation, adjusting to new environments over time, and their initial responses may differ significantly from their sustained experience. Therefore, studies must be long enough to allow for this adaptation and to observe behaviors and perceptions under typical, settled conditions.

Furthermore, maintenance schedules and the natural aging or wear of materials can subtly introduce confounding factors over long durations, requiring careful monitoring or planned interventions to ensure the purity of the experimental conditions.

If long-term temporal dynamics are not considered, studies may capture only fleeting effects, giving a false impression of a design's true performance over time. The "iterate quickly" philosophy that often underpins A/B testing in software development ultimately faces a fundamental challenge when confronted with "sticky" architectural interventions—design changes that are permanent, exceedingly difficult, or prohibitively expensive to revert. Architectural A/B testing, particularly for sticky interventions, demands an even higher degree of rigor in the pre-design and planning phases. It necessitates extensive simulation, prototyping, and small-scale testing *before* full-scale implementation. This reality reinforces the value of maximizing control and precision in every stage of the architectural A/B test, recognizing that the "undo" button is rarely an option in the built environment.

So, under what conditions are A/B tests most impactful? In the early-stage conceptual design, A/B testing might seem premature given the abstract nature of ideas. However, this is precisely where it can be most cost-effective. Architects can leverage simulations or mock-ups to conduct initial A/B tests. For instance, testing two different massing strategies for daylighting performance using computational models, or evaluating pedestrian flow patterns for two alternative plaza layouts in a virtual reality environment, allows for rapid iteration and comparison without any physical construction. This early application helps validate fundamental design hypotheses and identify promising directions before significant resources are committed; and helps narrow down directions in the early stages of a project in a low--cost environment. As design progresses into detailed design refinement, A/B testing continues to be invaluable. Here, more granular elements can be put to the test. This could involve using high-fidelity mock-ups of specific interior spaces (e.g., two different office workstation configurations) to gather occupant feedback on comfort or perceived privacy, or deploying sensor-based A/B tests on prototype facades to compare thermal performance under controlled conditions. At this stage, A/B testing helps optimize specific components and systems, ensuring that material choices, lighting strategies, or spatial arrangements achieve their intended effects.

Many firms find the greatest immediate value in A/B testing specific, high-cost decisions early on. Consider a commercial firm designing a new lobby space where a key design feature is a reception desk clad in either highly polished marble (Condition A) or matte, locally sourced wood (Condition B). The firm's hypothesis is that Condition B will be perceived as more "approachable" by visitors. Rather than committing to one expensive material, the firm's in-house research team or a student intern can construct two identical, medium-sized, high-fidelity mock-ups of the desk area in an empty conference room, differing *only* by the cladding material. They could then randomly assign a group of potential end-users (e.g., employees from the client's office or even people recruited from the street) to view either Mock-up A or Mock-up B, and then immediately administer a short survey asking them to rate the perceived "approachability" on a 7-point Likert scale. This simple, randomized setup provides a causally clean answer—often for the cost of a few sheets of veneer and a pizza lunch—to a question that would otherwise be left to a subjective debate between the design partner and the client.

In post-occupancy evaluation (POE), A/B testing can be instrumental for assessing the real-world performance of complete architectural interventions. This might involve comparing two different operational modes within a building (e.g., varying HVAC setpoints between two identical zones) or evaluating the long-term impact of a design change introduced in one part of a campus versus another. POE-based A/B tests provide crucial feedback on actual building performance and user behavior, informing future projects and validating initial design goals. However, meticulous attention must be paid to ensuring the "identicality" of the environments being compared. While the ideal A/B test necessitates that conditions A and B differ only by the specific design intervention being studied, achieving such perfect equivalence in real-world architectural settings is exceptionally challenging. Factors like subtle variations in building orientation, adjacent site conditions, occupant demographics, or even historical usage patterns can introduce confounding variables, obscuring the true effect of the design change. Consequently, researchers must either carefully select spaces that are as closely matched as possible, or employ robust statistical methods to control for these unavoidable differences, thereby mitigating threats to internal validity and strengthening the confidence in any causal inferences drawn from the architectural A/B test.

For optimal deployment of A/B testing in architecture, particularly to mitigate the challenges of "stickiness" and "occupant adaptation," researchers should strongly consider focusing on transient environments—spaces that people primarily pass through rather than occupy for extended periods. This strategic choice offers several significant advantages that align well with the core principles of A/B testing. Firstly, the short duration of exposure in transient spaces inherently minimizes occupant adaptation effects. Unlike long-term environments where users might habituate to a design or change their behaviors over time, transient settings capture more immediate, intuitive responses. This allows the A/B test to more directly measure initial perceptions, aesthetic appeal, wayfinding clarity, or immediate emotional responses, which are often the primary objectives for such spaces.

Secondly, these environments significantly reduce "stickiness" challenges. Since the intervention is typically experienced briefly and does not involve permanent residence, the logistical and financial barriers to swapping out design elements or reverting to a control condition for different participant groups or time periods are substantially lower than in, say, a residential or office setting. This facilitates cleaner randomization and more controlled experimental exposure. Thirdly, randomization itself is often more straightforward to implement. Researchers can often employ time-based randomization (e.g., alternating conditions by day or hour), or spatial randomization across multiple similar units, without disrupting long-term occupants. Finally, the typical outcomes measured in transient environments—such as immediate wayfinding efficiency, attention capture, traffic flow patterns, or initial perceived spaciousness—are well-suited to the strengths of A/B testing, being observable and quantifiable over short periods. This makes transient spaces an ideal proving ground for architectural A/B tests seeking robust and actionable insights.

To illustrate the principles of A/B testing in a tangible architectural context, let us consider a common challenge in large public buildings: efficient wayfinding. Imagine a newly designed contemporary art museum featuring a grand, multi-level atrium that serves as the primary entry and circulation hub. While aesthetically striking, initial observations suggest visitors are frequently disoriented when trying to locate specific galleries. The museum management wants to implement a signage system that improves visitor navigation, and they are considering two distinct design approaches:

The core problem is visitor disorientation and inefficient wayfinding in the museum atrium. The design team hypothesizes that a strategically designed digital signage system (Condition B) will significantly improve wayfinding efficiency compared to the existing static, minimalist signage (Condition A).

- *Condition A (Control)*: The existing wayfinding system, comprising discreet, static text-based signs at key decision points, integrated subtly into the architectural surfaces. This serves as our baseline.
- *Condition B (Treatment)*: A newly proposed digital signage system. This involves large, dynamic LED screens displaying real-time information, interactive maps, and animated directional cues, strategically placed at prominent vertical circulation points and intersections within the atrium. This is the independent variable being manipulated.

To ensure a valid comparison, the museum decides to conduct a randomized A/B test over several weeks, leveraging the transient nature of the atrium environment which minimizes long-term occupant adaptation and circumvents the "stickiness" of permanent structural changes. Given the constant flow of diverse visitors, direct individual randomization is impractical. Instead, the A/B test will employ a counterbalanced time-based randomization strategy:

- For Week 1, specific operating days (e.g., Tuesdays, Thursdays, Saturdays) will have Condition A (static signage) active, while the remaining operating days (e.g., Wednesdays, Fridays, Sundays) will have Condition B (digital signage) active.
- For Week 2, this schedule will be reversed: the days previously assigned to Condition A will now have Condition B active, and vice versa. This alternating pattern will continue for the duration of the study (e.g., 4–6 weeks).

By systematically swapping the conditions across days of the week, this approach effectively controls for potential confounding variables such as inherent day-of--week differences in visitor demographics, traffic volume, or staff presence. This method strengthens the internal validity of the test, ensuring that any observed differences are truly attributable to the signage design. A robust test duration encompassing multiple weeks accounts for broader temporal trends and ensures adequate sample size and statistical power to detect a meaningful effect. It also serves to ensure that the sample size is sufficiently large.

In this museum wayfinding study, the design team aims to detect a 30-second reduction in the average wayfinding time, considering this a practically significant improvement in visitor experience. Assuming a standard significance level (α) of 0.05 (corresponding to a Z-value of 1.96 for a two-tailed test), a desired statistical power of 80% (corresponding to a Z-value of 0.84), and an estimated standard deviation (σ) of 40 s for wayfinding times (derived from pilot observations or historical data), the required sample size per condition can be precisely calculated, using the standard formula earlier in this chapter:

$$\text{Sample Size} = \left(1.96 + 0.84\right)^2 * \left(2 * 40^2\right) / \left(30^2\right)$$

This results in approximately 28 observed visitors per condition. Therefore, to achieve 80% power in detecting a 30-second reduction with 95% confidence, the museum would need to track and collect data from roughly 28 visitors for the static signage condition (A) and 28 visitors for the digital signage condition (B), totaling a minimum required 56 visitor observations for the entire experiment. This calculation provides a clear, evidence-based target for the duration of the testing period, ensuring the study is adequately powered to yield statistically meaningful conclusions. Should the museum prefer 90% power, they would have a minimum of 76 participants. In real-world architectural settings, unexpected variability in visitor behavior, environmental conditions, or data collection issues (e.g., dropped observations) can easily exceed initial estimates. Therefore, 56 serve as the theoretical floor; in practice, collecting slightly more data can act as a safeguard against unforeseen complexities and increase the robustness of the conclusions.

To quantify "wayfinding efficiency," several measurable outcomes (dependent variables) may be collected using a combination of unobtrusive observation and technology:

1. *Time to Locate a Target Gallery*: Volunteer researchers, equipped with tablets, will unobtrusively track randomly selected visitors from the atrium entrance to a pre-designated "target gallery" (e.g., "The Modern Art Wing") and record the time taken. This provides a direct measure of efficiency.
2. *Number of Wayfinding Stops/Hesitations*: Researchers will also count how many times observed visitors stop, look around confusedly, or consult personal devices for directions during their journey to the target gallery. Fewer stops indicate better clarity.
3. *Self-Reported Wayfinding Confidence*: Brief, anonymous surveys administered by staff at the target gallery exit (after visitors have found it) will ask visitors to rate their confidence in navigating the atrium on a Likert scale. This captures perceived ease of use.
4. *Heatmap Data from Visitor Tracking (Optional)*: If the museum has existing indoor positioning technology (e.g., Wi-Fi analytics, camera-based tracking), heatmaps can visualize visitor flow and identify areas of congestion or hesitation under each signage condition, providing rich behavioral data.

After collecting data for the predetermined duration, the next step involves statistical analysis. For the "Time to Locate" and "Number of Stops" data (continuous outcomes), a *t*-test would be appropriate to compare the means between Condition A and Condition B. For the "Wayfinding Confidence" (ordinal/categorical data), a chi-square test or similar non-parametric test might be used. The null hypothesis (H_0) would state that there is no statistically significant difference in wayfinding efficiency or confidence between the static (A) and digital (B) signage systems. The alternative hypothesis (H_A) would propose that a significant difference *does* exist. If the analysis reveals that the p-value is below the chosen significance level (e.g., 0.05), the null hypothesis would be rejected. For instance, if visitors using the digital signage (B) consistently locate galleries significantly faster and with fewer hesitations than those using static signage (A), this provides strong empirical evidence that the digital system genuinely improves wayfinding. This result would indicate a meaningful average treatment effect (ATE).

While the museum atrium A/B test is designed to be robust, particularly benefiting from its transient environment and counterbalanced randomization, practical real-world experiments are rarely perfect. Several potential weaknesses could still influence the results, and considering their mitigation is crucial for enhancing the study's validity. Although the counterbalanced design helps control for regular day--of-week variations, it might not fully account for unpredictable or irregular events such as public holidays, sudden school closures, major local city events, or unannounced museum-specific programs (e.g., a special late-night viewing) that could dramatically alter visitor demographics, volume, or behavior on specific days. If such an event falls predominantly on days assigned to one condition, it could skew results. An experimentalist can mitigate these concerns by excluding days with known major deviations (e.g., official public holidays, major festivals) from the data collection, or by continuously monitoring daily visitor counts and anecdotal observations. If an unexpected event significantly impacts visitor patterns on a test day, consider excluding that day's data or collecting additional data to re-balance the sample. Running the experiment during a period where either both conditions experience similar holidays, or neither do, is optimal.

It's also important to consider how unobtrusive the volunteers observing visitors are. Visitors might consciously or subconsciously behave differently if they sense they are being watched, potentially influencing wayfinding patterns. This is known as the Hawthorne effect. Researchers can address this by training observers rigorously to blend in, maintain distance, and avoid direct eye contact. Observers should be dressed in inconspicuous clothing, and look like visitors themselves. Preferably, however, prioritizing automated tracking technologies wherever possible would reduce human presence and potential for bias.

The survey at the end should include questions, after the dependent variable questions are answered, about frequency of visits and prior visits. The museum may have a significant proportion of repeat visitors who are already familiar with its layout, regardless of the signage. Their wayfinding efficiency might not be truly influenced by the A/B test intervention, potentially diluting the observed effect or introducing noise. During analysis, a researcher can segment the data by "first-time visitors" vs. "repeat visitors" to see if the effect of the signage is more pronounced or different for novel users. By carefully considering the potential weaknesses of an experimental design in its early stages, researchers can proactively implement strategies to enhance its robustness and validity.

The architectural interpretation extends beyond just statistical numbers. A significant improvement in wayfinding efficiency directly enhances the visitor experience by reducing frustration, improving visitor flow, and potentially increasing the time spent engaging with exhibits rather than searching for them. Such data-driven insights empower the design team to confidently recommend the permanent installation of the digital signage system, not based on intuition or aesthetic preference, but on measurable, evidence-based performance.

A/B testing, at its heart, represents the most fundamental and accessible form of randomized control experimentation available to architectural researchers and practitioners. Its elegance lies in its simplicity: a direct comparison between two conditions—a control and a single, targeted intervention—underpinned by the power of random assignment. This chapter has laid bare the robust statistical framework that transforms intuitive design hunches into quantifiable insights, demonstrating how to precisely define hypotheses, determine appropriate sample sizes, and interpret results to confidently attribute observed outcomes to specific design choices.

While acknowledging the unique practicalities of the built environment, including the inherent "stickiness" of architectural interventions and the complexities of human adaptation, strategic applications have also been explored, particularly in transient spaces that mitigate these challenges. A/B testing empowers architects to move beyond mere aesthetics or convention, offering an empirical bedrock for refining designs, validating innovations, and ultimately, optimizing spaces for their occupants and purpose. It is through this systematic, two-group comparison that a clear understanding of what truly works is established. Having now mastered this basic yet extraordinarily powerful experimental methodology, the groundwork is laid to build upon these foundational principles and venture into the more intricate and multifaceted experimental designs necessary to unravel the complex interplay between people and the built environment.

References

Astachova, I. F., K. A. Makoviy, Yu V. Khitskova, and N. A. Burakova. "Information resources usability and split-testing features." In *Journal of Physics: Conference Series*, vol. 1479, no. 1, p. 012010. IOP Publishing, 2020.

Kohavi, Ron, and Roger Longbotham. "Online controlled experiments and A/B tests." *Encyclopedia of machine learning and data mining* (2015): 1–11.

Kohavi, Ron, Diane Tang, and Ya Xu. *Trustworthy online controlled experiments: A practical guide to a/b testing*. Cambridge University Press, 2020.

Steidl, Robert J., and Len Thomas. "Power analysis and experimental design." *Design and analysis of ecological experiments* 2 (2001): 415.

Xiang, Ding, Rebecca West, Jiaqi Wang, Xiquan Cui, and Jinzhou Huang. "Multi armed bandit vs. a/b tests in e-commerce-confidence interval and hypothesis test power perspectives." In *Proceedings of the 28th ACM SIGKDD conference on knowledge discovery and data mining*, pp. 4204–4214. 2022.

Chapter 4
Factorial Design: Managing Multiple Variables

Chapter Definitions

Main Effect

The independent impact of one independent variable on the dependent variable, averaged across all levels of the other factor(s).

Example: Participants rated rooms with 12ft ceilings as significantly more spacious than those with 8ft ceilings, demonstrating a main effect of ceiling height.

Interaction Effect

The effect of one independent variable on the dependent variable depends on the level of another independent variable, meaning the variables combine in a way that produces outcomes that wouldn't be predicted by examining each factor individually.

Example: The effect of lighting on comfort depended on ceiling height–task lighting improved comfort in high-ceiling rooms but reduced it in low-ceiling rooms–showing an interaction effect.

Factorial design experiments are a powerful tool for studying the effects of multiple independent variables on a dependent variable. Unlike traditional A/B testing, which compares only two conditions, factorial designs allow for the simultaneous manipulation of two or more factors, enabling researchers to explore not only the individual effects of each factor but also how these factors interact with one another. In architectural research, design decisions are rarely influenced by a single variable. While A/B testing is exceptionally effective for isolating the impact of one change (e.g., comparing two different door handles), the reality of built environments involves a complex interplay of elements. How a new material performs might depend on the lighting conditions; how people navigate a space could be influenced by both signage and spatial layout. A/B testing, in its singular focus, would require

C. J. Zolan, *Best Practice for Experimental Methods in Architecture*,
https://doi.org/10.1007/978-3-032-15884-0_4

multiple, disconnected experiments to explore these relationships, potentially missing the crucial synergistic or antagonistic effects between variables.

This is where factorial designs offer a significant leap forward. Their core strength lies in their ability to uncover interaction effects. An interaction occurs when the effect of one design element on an outcome changes depending on the level of another design element. For instance, a warm lighting temperature might make a small room feel cozy, but the same warm lighting in a very large room might make it feel dim and unwelcome. Here, the effect of "lighting temperature" interacts with "room size." Understanding such interactions is paramount in architecture, as it reflects the nuanced ways in which design components combine to shape human experience. Spaces are dynamic assemblages whose qualities cannot be fully understood by reducing them to isolated parts. Instead, interactions reveal non-additive effects that emerge from the combination of factors, providing richer explanatory power and predictive capacity.

Factorial designs are structured by combining the "levels" of each "factor" (independent variable). A common example is a 2×2 factorial design, involving two factors, each with two levels. This means that researchers can have multiple independent variables (Yates, 1937). Consider an architecture researcher studying how both ceiling height (Factor 1: 8 ft vs. 12 ft) and room lighting (Factor 2: ambient vs. task lighting) affect occupant comfort. This would result in four experimental conditions: ceiling height 8 ft with ambient lighting, ceiling height 8 ft with task lighting, ceiling height 12 ft with ambient lighting, and ceiling height 12 ft with task lighting. This is represented in tabular form in Fig. 4.1.

For a deeper understanding, interactions can be distinguished by their nature. In quantitative (or ordinal) interactions, the effect of one factor changes in magnitude (e.g., gets stronger or weaker) across the levels of another factor, but the direction of the effect remains consistent. For example, a specific material might always improve acoustic comfort, but its positive impact is significantly greater in a reverberant space compared to a dampened one. More profoundly, qualitative (or disordinal/crossover) Interactions occur when the direction of one factor's effect actually reverses across the levels of another factor. An example might be a specific type of seating arrangement (e.g., rigid, linear) that facilitates more effective collaboration in formal meeting rooms but actively hinders it in informal lounge areas, while an

	Task Lighting	Ambient Lighting
8ft Ceiling	*1*	*2*
12ft Ceiling	*3*	*4*

Fig. 4.1 Factorial design

alternative seating arrangement (e.g., modular, circular) shows the opposite pattern. Such interactions are critical because they dictate entirely different design recommendations based on contextual variables.

The presence of a significant interaction has profound implications for interpreting experimental results. A robust interaction often supersedes the interpretation of main effects. If two factors interact, their individual main effects, when considered in isolation, can be misleading; the true story lies in their combined influence. This highlights the contingent nature of design principles: optimal architectural solutions are rarely universal but are instead dependent on the specific combination of interacting factors. This understanding moves design theory beyond simplistic linear models towards more sophisticated, context-aware frameworks that reflect the complexity of real-world architectural challenges. Furthermore, factorial designs can reveal higher-order interactions, involving three or more factors (e.g., a three-way interaction between ceiling height, lighting type, and activity level). While these can be more challenging to visualize and interpret, they uncover even deeper, more subtle interdependencies among multiple design elements, offering the richest insights into complex architectural phenomena. By focusing on these synergistic and non-additive effects, researchers can move beyond reductionist analyses, fostering a holistic understanding of how built environments truly shape human experience and functional outcomes.

Conceptualizing Interaction Effects

Imagine you're holding a pair of Kings, usually a very strong hand. But then the flop comes down with an Ace showing. Because many players tend to play strong hands when an Ace is on the board, the value of your Kings decreases–it's riskier, since someone might have an Ace and beat you. Now your Kings aren't as powerful as they would be if the flop had no Ace.

In this analogy, the strength of your Kings (one independent variable) depends on whether an Ace is present in the flop (another independent variable). The interaction effect here means the value of your Kings changes based on the context of the flop. So, the "power of Kings" isn't fixed–it varies depending on the presence or absence of an Ace on the table.

Beyond interactions, factorial designs also allow us to measure main effects, which describe the overall impact of each independent variable on the outcome, averaged across all levels of the other variables. For example, a main effect of ceiling height might indicate that, on average, higher ceilings lead to a greater sense of spaciousness, regardless of the lighting type. By examining both main and interaction effects, researchers can develop a more comprehensive and accurate understanding of how architectural elements influence human behavior and perception. In factorial designs, however, it is important to check any main effects against the presence and nature of any interaction effects. While a main effect provides a valuable summary of a factor's overall influence, it represents an average across different conditions of other variables. If a significant interaction is present, the main effect alone can sometimes be misleading or incomplete, as the factor's influence may vary considerably across the levels of interacting variables. For instance, a main effect for "lighting type" might suggest that task lighting is generally preferred, but a significant interaction with "ceiling height" could reveal that task lighting is only preferred in 8 ft ceilings, and ambient lighting is preferred in 12 ft ceilings. In such cases, the interaction offers a more precise and actionable insight for design. It is important to note that the absence of a statistically significant main effect does not necessarily imply that a factor is inconsequential. A factor might not show a consistent overall influence on average, but its effect could still be critically important as part of a significant interaction.

A key feature of factorial design is the ability to examine interactions between factors. An interaction occurs when the effect of one factor on the outcome depends on the level of another factor. In the context of the architecture example, an interaction might arise if the impact of lighting on comfort changes depending on the ceiling height. This means that the effect of lighting alone cannot be fully understood without considering how it interacts with the ceiling height, and vice versa. The factorial design experiment can be conceptualized as a mathematical model where the independent variables (factors) are manipulated at different levels, and the effects of these manipulations on the dependent variable are measured. A simple example of a factorial design is a 2×2 design, where there are two factors, each with two levels. For instance, the first factor could be "ceiling height" with two levels (e.g., 8 ft and 12 ft), and the second factor could be "lighting type" with two levels (e.g., ambient and task lighting).

Mathematically, factorial designs can be represented in terms of the effects they measure. The fundamental goal is to determine the main effects and interaction effects. The main effect of a factor represents the average change in the outcome variable that is associated with different levels of that factor, averaged across the levels of the other factors. The interaction effect between two factors reveals whether the effect of one factor depends on the level of the other factor. Let's illustrate this using the example of a 2 × 2 factorial design, where Factor 1 is ceiling height (two levels, 8 ft and 12 ft) and Factor 2 is lighting type (two levels, ambient and task).

$$Y(1) = \text{Outcome for ceiling height } 8\,\text{ft}, \text{task lighting}$$

$$Y(2) = \text{Outcome for ceiling height } 8\,\text{ft}, \text{ambient lighting}$$

$$Y(3) = \text{Outcome for ceiling height } 12\,\text{ft}, \text{task lighting}$$

$$Y(4) = \text{Outcome for ceiling height } 12\,\text{ft}, \text{ambient lighting}$$

The goal is to assess the main effects and the interaction effect between the two factors. The main effect of ceiling height is the difference between the average of $Y(1)$ and $Y(2)$ (the outcomes at 8 ft ceiling) and the average of $Y(3)$ and $Y(4)$ (the outcomes at 12 ft ceiling). This is calculated as:

$$\text{Main Effect of Ceiling Height} = \left(\frac{Y(1)+Y(2)}{2}\right) - \left(\frac{Y(3)+Y(4)}{2}\right)$$

Similarly, the main effect of lighting type is the difference between the average of $Y(1)$ and $Y(3)$ (the outcomes with ambient lighting) and the average of $Y(2)$ and $Y(4)$ (the outcomes with task lighting):

$$\text{Main Effect of Lighting Height} = \left(\frac{Y(1)+Y(3)}{2}\right) - \left(\frac{Y(2)+Y(4)}{2}\right)$$

This interaction effect reveals whether the effect of one factor (e.g., lighting) depends on the level of the other factor (e.g., ceiling height). If the interaction effect is significant, it suggests that the impact of ceiling height on user comfort differs depending on the type of lighting used, and vice versa. It is calculated by subtracting the average of $Y(1)$ and $Y(2)$ from the average of $Y(3)$ and $Y(4)$, and then calculating the difference between the two:

$$\text{Interaction Effect} = (Y_1 - Y_2) - (Y_3 - Y_4)$$

If the interaction effect is close to zero, it indicates no significant interaction between the two factors, meaning the effect of one factor is not dependent on the other. If the interaction effect is large, it suggests that the two factors interact, and the effect of one factor is influenced by the level of the other factor. By calculating the main effects and the interaction effect, you can understand not only the independent effects of each factor but also how they work together to influence the dependent variable.

When implementing factorial designs, researchers must also consider how participants are assigned to these conditions. Factorial designs can be:

- *Between-Subjects Designs*: Where different groups of participants are exposed to each unique combination of factor levels. For example, one group of people experiences only the "8 ft ceiling with ambient lighting" condition.
- *Within-Subjects (Repeated Measures) Designs*: Where the same group of participants experiences all combinations of the factor levels. For instance, the same participants might experience all four of the ceiling height and lighting combinations.
- *Mixed Designs*: Which combine both between-subjects and within-subjects factors.

The ability of factorial designs to efficiently test multiple variables and, most importantly, uncover their interactions, makes them an indispensable tool for architectural researchers seeking to move beyond simple cause-and-effect relationships. While increasing the number of factors and levels can lead to a rapid increase in experimental conditions and analytical complexity, this complexity often mirrors the intricate reality of the built environment. Properly designed factorial experiments allow architects to generate nuanced, evidence-based insights that directly inform more effective and responsive designs.

The process of selecting factors and levels in factorial designs requires balancing theoretical relevance, ecological validity (how well experimental conditions reflect real-world settings), and methodological rigor with pragmatic constraints. This strategic selection underpins the ultimate validity, interpretability, and impact of factorial experiments in architectural research, ensuring studies are not only methodologically sound but also directly translatable to design practice. Firstly, factors should represent variables with substantive significance to architectural practice, rigorously grounded in prior empirical research, established design theory, or relevant psychological and social science frameworks. This theoretical justification ensures that chosen factors reflect specific constructs or address critical gaps in existing knowledge. It moves beyond arbitrary selections to focus on variables amenable to intervention within design practice and with a high probability of influencing human experience or building performance.

Secondly, levels for each factor must be chosen to reflect meaningful, realistic variations that are ecologically valid. For instance, selecting ceiling heights of 8 and 12 ft corresponds to common architectural standards, ensuring that results are interpretable and actionable within typical design parameters. Conversely, arbitrary or overly extreme levels, while sometimes scientifically interesting, may reduce external validity, making findings difficult to generalize to real-world contexts. Ecological validity exists on a spectrum; the choice of levels should align with the desired level of realism for the study, whether it's a controlled laboratory simulation or a full-scale field experiment. The variations between levels must also be sufficiently distinct to produce a detectable effect, avoiding situations where the chosen levels are too similar or too extreme to show any further impact.

Statistical considerations impose critical limits on the number of factors and levels. Each additional factor multiplies the total experimental conditions exponentially. For example, moving from a 2×2 (4 conditions) to a 2×2×2 (8 conditions) to a 2×2×2×2 (16 conditions) can quickly lead to a large number of cells. This exponential growth can significantly dilute statistical power if sample sizes are not increased proportionally, making it difficult to detect genuine effects, especially subtle interactions. Therefore, conducting an a priori power analysis becomes essential to determine the necessary sample size required to detect anticipated effect sizes. Moreover, factors chosen should ideally be conceptually and empirically independent (orthogonal, statistically independent from one another) to allow for clear and unambiguous interpretation of main and interaction effects while acknowledging that perfect orthogonality is rare in complex architectural contexts, designs should minimize unintended correlations.

Factorial designs, particularly those involving three or more factors, require a level of methodological control and statistical analysis that often exceeds the capacity of an in-house architecture team. This complexity is why academic-practice partnerships are the gold standard for executing these experiments. The university researcher contributes expertise in experimental rigor (e.g., proper randomization techniques, statistical power analysis, and robust interpretation of complex interaction terms) and often provides access to controlled, simulated environments (e.g., VR labs or dedicated mock-up facilities). The architectural firm contributes *e*cological validity (providing real-world design problems, realistic factor levels, and domain-specific knowledge) and often provides the necessary funding or in-kind construction materials for mock-ups.

For instance, testing a 2×2×2 design on a new façade system (comparing Shading Depth, Window-to-Wall Ratio and Material Finish) requires sophisticated instrumentation to measure thermal performance (the dependent variable, Y) and meticulous control over solar exposure—a task best handled by a university's building science lab. The firm benefits from a causally validated façade design; the academic partner gains publishable research. This symbiotic relationship ensures that the complexity of factorial design is managed efficiently, leading to high-quality, actionable, and theoretically rich evidence.

Factorial designs represent a vital advancement for architectural research, moving beyond the singular focus of A/B testing to embrace the inherent multi-dimensionality of the built environment. Their capacity to simultaneously explore the influence of multiple design elements, and critically, to uncover the complex interaction effects between them, provides an unparalleled depth of insight into how spaces are truly experienced and utilized.

Reference

Yates, Frank. "The design and analysis of factorial experiments." (1937).

Chapter 5
Within-Subjects Design: Understanding Individual Responses

Chapter Definitions

Statistical Power

The probability of correctly rejecting a false null hypothesis when it is, in fact, false

Example: When evaluating whether a new hospital layout reduces medical errors—a high-stakes outcome—you'd want high statistical power, whereas testing preferences for paint color in a waiting room could tolerate lower power due to lower consequence of error.

Hypothesis

A testable statement that proposes a relationship between two or more variables.

Example: Buildings with symmetrical, monumental facades elicit greater perceived state authority than asymmetrical or minimalist designs.

When determining the type of factorial design of an experiment, it is important to consider how much the "noise" of individual differences is in the end product of focus. In many areas of architectural research, the subtle nuances of human experience and behavior are paramount, and these can easily be obscured by the inherent variability between different people. This is precisely where within-subjects design offers a powerful solution. By exposing the same participants to all the experimental conditions, this methodology allows researchers to effectively control for individual differences, transforming each participant into their own internal control. This fundamental shift means that any observed changes in response are more likely attributable to the manipulated architectural variables, rather than pre-existing individual characteristics. The profound advantage of this approach lies in its ability to dramatically reduce inter-individual variability within the data, thereby sharpening the statistical precision of the experiment. This increased statistical power makes within-subjects designs particularly adept at detecting even subtle yet significant

C. J. Zolan, *Best Practice for Experimental Methods in Architecture*,
https://doi.org/10.1007/978-3-032-15884-0_5

effects of the built environment that might otherwise be masked by noise in a between-subjects comparison.

Consider for a moment, a Holocaust Museum. A Holocaust Museum, above all, must resonate not as a collective abstraction, but as a crucible for individual human understanding, where each visitor's unique journey through its spaces becomes a deeply personal act of witness and remembrance. At the design stage, a within-group experimental design is the most appropriate vehicle to ensure consideration of the immense and highly personal variability in individual baselines—from emotional resilience and personal history to sensitivity and traumatic content. This is achieved by carefully designing the museum as a sequence of distinct architectural conditions, such as transitions from oppressive confinement to moments of quiet contemplation, or specific light and soundscapes. Researchers can then expose each individual visitor to these varied experiential zones. This approach controls for the inherent "noise" that would arise if different groups were compared, allowing for precise measurement of how that specific individual's physiological responses (e.g., heart rate variability indicating stress), emotional self-reports, or cognitive engagement (e.g., reflection depth) change as they navigate each designed segment. Such precision is crucial to understanding the effectiveness of the architectural narrative, enabling architects to discern which specific spatial elements or transitions reliably elicit the intended emotional arc or transformative experience within individuals, rather than merely observing average group differences that might obscure the true, deeply personal impact of the design.

When designing a memorial or commemorative space, the goal is not just a single effect (like low stress) but a carefully orchestrated emotional trajectory. A research team wishes to test how two fundamental architectural decisions—the path taken and the material finish—interact to influence the visitor's sense of compression and emotional state. They set up a 2×2 factorial experiment using a large, controlled prototype. The first factor is Path Geometry (G), with two levels: a G_1 Linear Path (forced, narrow, non-divergent route) versus a G_2 Meandering Path (wider, curving, offering small moments of choice). The second factor is Materiality (M), with M_1 being Rough Concrete (cold, heavy, perceived as permanent) and M_2 being Oiled Steel (dark, reflective, perceived as transient/industrial). This design creates four distinct, randomly assigned conditions, ranging from the Linear Path/Rough Concrete combination to the Meandering Path/Oiled Steel combination. The dependent variables (Y) could be the change in perceived compression (a survey score) and emotional valence (measured physiologically via Galvanic Skin Response, or GSR, indicating arousal).

The interaction effect here is the critical discovery. For instance, the research might reveal that a Linear Path (G_1) maximizes "Perceived Compression" only when combined with the cold, heavy feel of Rough Concrete (M_1). Conversely, the Meandering Path (G_2) might lose its slightly "lighter" feel when executed in Oiled Steel (M_2) because the reflectivity amplifies the sense of being enclosed. This is a design insight—that the path geometry's intended effect depends entirely on the chosen material—that no simple A/B test could ever provide.

The choice of a within-subjects design here is not merely for statistical efficiency; it is a methodological necessity rooted in ethical and design intent. The population interacting with such a memorial often includes individuals who are personally or ancestrally impacted by the trauma, meaning their baseline emotional resilience and physiological responses are inherently high variance and highly sensitive. If the museum were tested using a between-subjects approach—where one group experienced the Confining Space and a *different* group experienced the Expansive Space—the resulting data would be statistically unusable for this purpose. Only by measuring the intrapersonal change—the shift in Y_1 and Y_2 within the same individual—can the researcher confidently assert that the architectural transition *caused* the observed change in stress, regardless of that individual's unique, high-noise baseline.

The inherent efficiency of within-subjects designs directly addresses the real-world constraints of architectural practice and the high-stakes nature of the environment. Because each participant serves as their own control, the experiment requires a significantly smaller sample size to achieve the same statistical power compared to a between-subjects study. This dramatically reduces the burden on the architectural firm or museum, easing logistical constraints related to recruitment, privacy, and security—especially vital in sensitive environments like a Holocaust museum where participant pool access is limited and ethical protection is paramount. By yielding high statistical power with low sample count, the design aligns methodological rigor with practical necessity.

Within-subjects experimental designs allow for the testing of effects of different variables within the same group of participants. The primary strength of a within-subjects design is that each participant serves as their own control, which reduces variability caused by individual differences (Charness et al., 2012). This allows for more precise measurements of how the experimental variables influence outcomes. In a within-subjects design, every participant will experience all of these conditions in a controlled, randomized order, often leading to greater internal validity (Birnbrauer, 1981). This is because all participants are exposed to the same set of conditions, which ensures that any observed differences in outcomes are more likely due to the experimental manipulation rather than differences in individual characteristics. This greater internal validity strengthens the ability to draw causal inferences, a key aspect of experimental research, making it easier to attribute changes in behavior, perception, or performance to specific design features rather than uncontrolled variables. Theoretical generalization is enhanced in a within-subjects design. Since each participant serves as their own control, the conclusions drawn from the study are often more robust and can be more easily generalized to broader architectural contexts.

For example, let's again consider a study where a researcher wishes to investigate the impact of two lighting conditions (ambient and task lighting) and two ceiling heights (8 ft and 12 ft) on the comfort and productivity of individuals working in an office space. The design would require that each participant experience all four combinations of these factors—8 ft with ambient lighting, 8 ft with task lighting, 12 ft with ambient lighting, and 12 ft with task lighting. By comparing the same individual's reactions across different conditions, the effects of individual differences such as age, prior experience, and preferences are minimized. In the context of this within-subjects design, the analysis typically focuses on differences in responses within each participant across different conditions. You would calculate the change in perceived comfort or productivity between conditions, and then average these differences across participants. For each participant, the difference in outcome (comfort or productivity) between conditions can be written as:

$$D_{ij} = Y_{ij} - Y_{i0}$$

where

- D_{ij} is the difference in outcome for participant i between condition j (e.g., ambient lighting vs. task lighting at a ceiling height of 8 ft).
- Y_{ij} is the outcome for participant i in condition j.
- Y_{i0} is the outcome for participant i in the baseline or reference condition (such as their outcome in the first condition they experience).

Once these differences are calculated for all participants across conditions, the average difference across participants for each condition can be computed. This allows you to determine how significant the effect of the design features (e.g., ceiling height and lighting) is across the entire group. Mathematically, the average difference for condition j can be expressed as:

$$\text{Avg}\left(D_j\right) = \frac{1}{N}\sum_{i=1}^{N} D_{ij}$$

where

- N is the total number of participants.
- D_{ij} represents the individual differences for each participant in each condition.

Additionally, within-subjects designs require careful attention to the order of conditions. To control for potential order effects, you may randomize the order in which participants experience the different conditions. This minimizes any bias that could result from the sequence of conditions (such as fatigue or learning effects). In some cases, counterbalancing methods can be used, where different groups of participants experience different orders of conditions to ensure that each condition is tested in each position across participants. These methods are discussed in more detail later in this chapter.

Once the experimental data is collected, the next step is typically to analyze it using a repeated-measures analysis. This is because the same participants are being measured multiple times across conditions, creating a dependency between measurements. A common method for analyzing repeated-measures data is using a repeated-measures ANOVA. In this type of analysis, the model accounts for the fact that measurements from the same participant are not independent, as they are correlated. The basic formula for repeated-measures ANOVA is:

$$Y_{ij} = \mu + \alpha_j + \pi_i + \varepsilon_{ij}$$

where

- Y_{ij} is the outcome for participant i in condition j.
- μ is the overall mean of the data.
- α_j is the effect of condition j (such as the effect of lighting or ceiling height).
- π_i is the random effect of participant iii (accounts for individual differences).
- ϵ_{ij} is the error term, representing the variation that cannot be explained by the conditions or participant differences.

ANOVA, whether between-subject or repeated measures, partitions the total variability in the outcome variable (Y) into components attributable to the main effects of each factor and their interactions (St and Wold, 1989). The null hypothesis in a factorial ANOVA generally asserts that there are no differences due to any factor or their interactions. When the calculated p-value falls below a predetermined significance level (commonly 0.05), this indicates sufficient evidence to reject the null hypothesis, concluding that the factor or interaction significantly influences the outcome. This model allows you to assess whether there are significant differences in outcomes between conditions while controlling for the within-participant variability. A significant result would suggest that at least one of the experimental conditions had a different impact on the dependent variable.

Within-subject (repeated-measures) ANOVA makes several specific assumptions beyond those required for between-subject analyses. Most notably, it assumes sphericity—that the variances of the differences between all pairs of conditions are equal—and often compound symmetry, which requires equal variances across conditions and equal covariances between condition pairs. These assumptions reflect the correlated nature of repeated measurements taken from the same participant and are critical because violations can inflate the risk of Type I errors. Additionally, while observations must be independent across participants, measurements within the same participant are expected to be correlated, which the model explicitly accounts for.

Conceptualizing Sphericity

Early on in a multi-round poker tournamnet, you might be playing against players of similar or lower skill, so your experience and performance feel steady across rounds. But as the tournament goes on and weaker players get eliminated, the competition sharpens. You might face a less experienced player in one round and a tough pro the next. This changing level of difficulty means that your performance can swing dramatically from one round to another. This inconsistency in challenge is what breaks sphericity, making it harder to judge your true skill or progress based purely on the results.

If a player ignores sphericity, they risk attributing the drop in their poker wins to a decline in skill or bad luck, rather than the reality that the opponents are simply stronger as the tournament progresses.

As sphericity is often violated in practice given the exposure to multiple conditions, corrections such as Greenhouse–Geisser or Huynh-Feldt adjustments are frequently applied to maintain valid inference. These adjustments are crucial for preventing an inflated Type I error rate that would otherwise occur when sphericity is violated. They work by calculating a "sphericity epsilon" value, which quantifies the degree of the violation, and then applying this correction factor to the degrees of freedom used in the ANOVA's F-test. This process effectively makes the statistical test more conservative, counteracting the original inflation of the F-statistic. By doing so, these adjustments ensure that the resulting p-value more accurately reflects the true probability of observing the data under the null hypothesis, thereby safeguarding the trustworthiness and validity of the research findings.

Despite these challenges, within-subject design is ideal for experiments where only a small number of participants can take part, for practical or funding reasons, because each participant serves as their own control. This means variability between participants is reduced. This leads to more reliable results and a higher probability of detecting significant effects with fewer participants compared to a between-subjects design while also getting the same level of statistical power. This is also important for subtle architectural interventions, which may be missed in between-subject designs, because the reduced variability between participants means it can more easily detect small or subtle effects that might ordinarily be overlooked.

One important element of designing within-subject experiments is the introduction of washout periods. Sometimes, the effect of one condition might carry over into the next. For instance, participants exposed to a particular room design or lighting condition might have their perceptions or behaviors influenced by the first experience when they encounter the second condition. This is particularly relevant in architectural experiments, where physical or environmental factors could have lingering effects. In addition, because each participant is exposed to multiple conditions, they may become tired or bored, especially if the experiment takes a long time. This can affect the quality of their responses or behaviors, introducing noise into the data. Washout periods, the methodological term for a break between conditions, helps address this by giving participants time to return to a baseline state, reducing the influence of any lingering effects from the previous condition (Handley et al., 2018; (Savage and Waldman, 2008).

Conceptualizing Washout Periods

Imagine you're playing in a long poker game. After a tough few rounds where you lost a big hand and made risky plays, you might feel frustrated or distracted going into the next round–this state is known as tilt in poker, where emotions cloud your judgment. A washout period is like taking a break between these rounds–time to clear your head, reset your mindset, and shake off any lingering bad luck or emotional baggage before jumping back in. Without this break, your judgment might be clouded, causing you to carry over past frustrations and make poor decisions. In experimental terms, a washout period lets any effects from one condition "fade away" so they don't influence how you perform or react in the next condition, ensuring each round is a fresh start.

It's important to consider the potential for carryover effects when determining the washout period and to ensure that it's long enough to allow for proper recovery, but not so long that participant fatigue or boredom sets in again (Tourangeau et al., 1989). Despite the potential use of washout periods, within-subjects designs are not appropriate for research that involves irreversible effects within the study. For example, if you're studying a condition that leaves a permanent change in the participant (e.g., exposure to a stressful environment), they cannot be exposed to future conditions fairly. Similarly, experiments involving physical or long-lasting mental changes might not be suitable for within-subjects designs. Such effects may confound results if not adequately addressed. These include practice effects (where performance improves due to familiarity with the task), fatigue effects (where performance declines due to boredom or exhaustion), interference effects (where exposure to one condition negatively impacts performance on a subsequent one), and sensitization (where participants become increasingly aware of the manipulation over time). Understanding these specific effects leads to a more nuanced appreciation of why rigorous counterbalancing strategies are so critical.

To address these, researchers primarily rely on counterbalancing, a systematic approach to varying the order in which participants experience the different experimental conditions. By randomizing the sequence of conditions for each participant, or by employing more sophisticated techniques like Latin Square designs, the aim is to distribute any potential carryover effects evenly across all conditions. This means that if, for instance, participants experience an improvement due to practice, or a decline due to fatigue, this effect is spread across all conditions, rather than disproportionately impacting one, allowing researchers to isolate the true effect of the architectural manipulation.

Latin Square designs, in particular, refer to designing exposure in such a way that each condition appears in every ordinal position (e.g., first, second, third exposure) an equal number of times across participants. Moreover, it guarantees that each condition precedes and follows every other condition exactly once (or as evenly as possible), thereby balancing out the various practice, fatigue, interference, and sensitization effects across the different conditions. It is particularly valuable because it allows researchers to manage carryover effects without having to administer every single possible sequence of conditions, which can quickly become impractical as the number of conditions increases. When proposing an experiment to a firm or client, the need for counterbalancing (like a Latin Square design) must be clearly explained. It is not sufficient to simply run the conditions in one fixed order. Practitioners must stress that counterbalancing is the insurance policy against concluding that the fatigue from the nth condition is actually a negative effect of the design. This ensures methodological integrity—the ability to *truly* attribute an outcome to the design.

In architectural experiments, where the physical environment or design features are often central to the study, participants may unintentionally form expectations about the conditions they are being exposed to. For example, if the experiment involves testing different types of lighting or room layouts, participants might realize that the purpose is to assess their preferences for light or spatial arrangements. This awareness can alter their behavior or responses, especially if they want to appear consistent with what they perceive as the experimenter's expectations or if they assume that their answers will influence the outcome. One way to mitigate this risk is by generalizing the purpose of the study. In some cases, this can be done by providing a cover story that aligns with the design conditions but doesn't directly indicate the research question. For example, if the study aims to assess how different room layouts affect social interaction, the cover story might focus on testing different "furniture arrangements for comfort" without revealing that the core research goal is to examine how space impacts social behavior. This makes it less likely that participants will adjust their responses based on their knowledge of the experimental manipulations. It is ordinarily not appropriate to mislead participants about the purpose of the study entirely.

In addition to masking the purpose, it's crucial that the conditions themselves are not so obvious that participants can easily guess what is being tested. If the manipulation is overly apparent, participants may alter their behavior to match what they believe is expected of them. For instance, if you're testing the impact of different noise levels in a workspace, participants might be aware that the noise is a primary factor influencing their focus or stress levels, leading them to artificially inflate or downplay their responses. To avoid this, it's essential to design the experiment so that the manipulations are subtle enough to avoid detection, or participants should be distracted with tasks that limit their focus on the experimental conditions.

A mandatory part of within-subjects design, as earlier referenced, is ensuring that the conditions are randomized or counterbalanced is another strategy to reduce bias. By altering the order in which participants experience the different conditions, you reduce the likelihood of them becoming aware of the manipulation based on a repetitive pattern or sequencing of experiences. This randomization or counterbalancing approach helps maintain the integrity of the data by ensuring that each participant is exposed to the full range of conditions without any predictable patterns emerging.

Despite their considerable strengths, within-subjects designs present a distinct set of challenges and inherent weaknesses that demand careful consideration. In a within-subjects design, participants experience multiple, often highly controlled, architectural conditions in a sequential manner that rarely mirrors real-world interaction with environments. This repeated exposure can lead to an artificiality where participants may become overly sensitized to the experimental manipulations or develop expectations about the study's purpose, potentially altering their natural responses. Consequently, while the findings may precisely describe how the same individual responds across controlled conditions, their generalizability to broader, more fluid, and less observed architectural contexts can be limited. Should these results then be directly applied to a different, uncontrolled architectural environment, there is a significant risk that the intended design outcomes—be they improved comfort, enhanced performance, or specific emotional responses—will simply not materialize, potentially leading to wasted resources and even unintended negative consequences for occupants. The tight control that enhances internal validity sometimes comes at the cost of ecological realism, requiring careful consideration when extrapolating results to actual design practice.

Participant attrition, or drop-out, represents another critical vulnerability. Since within-subjects designs typically require participants to commit to multiple sessions or extended periods, the increased time and effort burden makes them inherently more susceptible to participants withdrawing from the study compared to single-session, between-subjects designs. The impact of attrition is twofold: not only does it directly reduce the final sample size, thus diminishing statistical power, but more critically, if the drop-out is not random (e.g., participants who found certain architectural conditions particularly stressful or fatiguing choose to leave), the remaining sample becomes biased. This introduces a form of selection bias that can severely compromise the representativeness of the data and undermine the generalizability of any conclusions, even those drawn from internally valid within-participant comparisons.

Within-subjects designs also face fundamental limitations when dealing with irreversible effects or conditions that cause permanent changes. If an architectural manipulation, such as prolonged exposure to a highly disorienting or psychologically demanding space, fundamentally alters a participant's baseline state or induces a lasting psychological impact, subsequent conditions cannot be fairly assessed against an unchanged internal control. Similarly, experiments involving skills learning where knowledge cannot be "unlearned" are unsuitable. This constraint significantly restricts the range of architectural phenomena that can be ethically and practically studied using this design, compelling researchers to carefully consider the nature of their interventions and their potential for lasting, non-reversible impacts on participants. For instance, a study designed to measure the impact of an architectural space engineered to induce severe sensory deprivation or extreme psychological discomfort would be entirely inappropriate for a within-subjects approach. Once a participant has experienced profound psychological distress or disorientation in such a "stress" condition, their baseline emotional state and perception of subsequent, milder architectural environments would be fundamentally and irreversibly altered by the preceding trauma. It would be impossible to ascertain the true effect of a "calming" room, for example, if the participant's perception is still heavily skewed by lingering anxiety or a newly formed aversion, thus invalidating any comparative data collected within that individual.

References

Birnbrauer, Jay S. "External validity and experimental investigation of individual behaviour." *Analysis and Intervention in Developmental Disabilities* 1, no. 2 (1981): 117–132.

Charness, Gary, Uri Gneezy, and Michael A. Kuhn. "Experimental methods: Between-subject and within-subject design." *Journal of Economic Behavior & Organization* 81, no. 1 (2012): 1–8.

Handley, Margaret A., Courtney R. Lyles, Charles McCulloch, and Adithya Cattamanchi. "Selecting and improving quasi-experimental designs in effectiveness and implementation research." *Annual Review of Public Health* 39, no. 1 (2018): 5–25.

Savage, Scott J., and Donald M. Waldman. "Learning and fatigue during choice experiments: a comparison of online and mail survey modes." *Journal of Applied Econometrics* 23, no. 3 (2008): 351–371.

St, Lars, and Svante Wold. "Analysis of variance (ANOVA)." *Chemometrics and Intelligent Laboratory Systems* 6, no. 4 (1989): 259–272.

Tourangeau, Roger, Kenneth A. Rasinski, Norman Bradburn, and Roy D'Andrade. "Carryover effects in attitude surveys." *Public Opinion Quarterly* 53, no. 4 (1989): 495–524.

Chapter 6
Between-Subjects Design: Testing Different Groups

Chapter Definitions

Homogeneity of Variance

The assumption that the different groups or conditions in an experiment have roughly equal levels of variability in their scores or outcomes.

Example: In a study comparing acoustic comfort across three materials, each material's ratings are clustered similarly around their own average, even if the averages themselves differ.

When seeking to understand how different architectural choices truly resonate with people, sometimes the clearest insights emerge from distinct, unmixed comparisons. This is the essence of a between-subjects experimental design. This approach carefully assigns different groups of participants to each unique version of a design stimulus. Each person sees only one "story" or "image" of the built environment, ensuring their responses are a pure, untainted reaction, free from the biases of memory or direct comparison that might arise from experiencing alternatives. This method proves invaluable precisely when the "treatment"—be it a visual representation of a space, a detailed description of a material, or a conceptual layout—is meant to evoke an immediate, uninfluenced impression, or when the sheer scale of the manipulation makes repeated exposure impractical.

Consider, for example, a survey experiment designed to assess public preference for two distinct approaches to sustainable building facades: one showcasing highly visible eco-technologies (like prominent solar panels and green walls), and the other employing bioclimatic principles that are subtly integrated into a more traditional aesthetic. If the same person were to rate both designs, their evaluation of the second might be heavily influenced by their immediate comparison to the first, or by a desire for consistency. A between-subjects design bypasses this. Researchers would randomly present one group of respondents with images and descriptions of the

C. J. Zolan, *Best Practice for Experimental Methods in Architecture*,
https://doi.org/10.1007/978-3-032-15884-0_6

technology-forward facade, while the other comparable group would see only the subtly integrated design. This allows for an unbiased assessment of each style's standalone appeal, perceived environmental benefit, or aesthetic resonance, providing architects with clear data on public reception without the confounding "noise" of direct, internal comparisons within each participant. It ensures the capture of genuine, un-prompted responses to distinct architectural visions.

The fundamental premise of a between-subjects design hinges on the comparison of different groups, each exposed to a unique experimental condition. For any observed differences in outcomes to be confidently attributed to the architectural manipulations, these groups must be as equivalent as possible at the outset of the experiment. This initial comparability is paramount because, unlike within-subject designs where individual differences are controlled by repeated measures, in between-subjects designs, such differences constitute the primary source of "noise" that could obscure the true effect of the independent variable. The cornerstone method for achieving this initial equivalence is random assignment, and high-quality random assignment is at its most critical in between-subject design. Practical methods for random assignment in architectural survey experiments can vary. A simple approach might involve using a random number generator to assign participants to conditions as they join the study. For instance, if you have two conditions, participants might be assigned to condition A if the number is odd, and condition B if it's even. More sophisticated techniques, like block randomization, ensure that an equal number of participants are assigned to each condition after a certain block of enrollments (e.g., ensuring an equal number of participants in each condition after every four participants recruited).

There is some attention given to stratified randomization. This involves dividing the sample into strata based on the characteristic (e.g., sex) and then performing random assignment within each stratum. This approach is particularly useful when dealing with small to medium sample sizes where simple randomization might, by chance, lead to imbalances that confound results. However, while stratified randomization enhances internal validity by accounting for known covariates, it is not without complications. First, its effectiveness depends entirely on the researcher's ability to identify the most relevant confounding variables ahead of time. Unknown or unmeasured variables will not be balanced and may still bias outcomes. This is a serious concern, as latent structure can unintentionally introduce hidden biases or reinforce existing patterns in the data. That is, in seeking to "balance" one variable, the method may inadvertently unbalance another, unmeasured one. The illusion of control can lead to overconfidence in the fairness of group assignment, when in reality the process may be subtly shaped by unseen factors. Second, as the number of stratification factors increases, the sample can become fragmented into too many subgroups, each too small to reliably randomize — a problem known as overstratification. This is especially problematic in situations where recruiting large, uniform samples is impractical. Third, unless the stratification variables are accounted for during analysis, the statistical gains of the design can be lost, or worse, the results misinterpreted.

The reliance on distinct groups for each condition in a between-subjects design yields several significant advantages, making it the preferred or even the only feasible choice for certain types of architectural experiments. Primarily, this design completely eliminates the risk of carryover effects. Since each participant experiences only one architectural stimulus, there is no possibility of a previous exposure influencing their response to a subsequent one. This ensures that observed outcomes are genuine, uninfluenced reactions to the specific design, which is critical when assessing immediate impressions or isolated aesthetic judgments. Consequently, issues like practice effects (where performance improves with repetition) or fatigue effects (where performance declines due to boredom or exhaustion) are rendered irrelevant. Participants are also less likely to infer the study's hypothesis (reducing demand characteristics), as they are not exposed to the variations that might reveal the researcher's intent. Between-subjects designs are uniquely suited for investigating architectural manipulations that induce irreversible effects—such as exposure to a significantly traumatic space, or a profound learning experience—where it would be unethical or impossible for the same individual to return to a baseline state for another condition.

So why not design every experiment as a between-subject factorial design? At first glance, it appears to address many of the shortcomings associated with A/B testing and within-subject designs: it avoids carryover effects, minimizes participant fatigue, and allows for clean comparisons across multiple variables. However, the trade-offs are substantial. The most significant drawback is its inherently lower statistical power per participant. Because each group is composed of different individuals, the variability introduced by individual differences—including background, preferences, and prior experience—inflates the error variance. As a result, detecting an effect of a given size typically requires much larger sample sizes compared to within-subject designs. This increase in sample size directly impacts recruitment demands, time required for data collection, and overall study complexity. For architectural research in particular—where participants may be specialists, stakeholders, or users drawn from narrow populations—this logistical burden can quickly become prohibitive. This also increases the impact of attrition. In between-subject factorial designs, if participants drop out, entire cells (i.e., specific combinations of factor levels) can become unbalanced or underpowered. Since each participant contributes data to only one condition, their loss directly weakens that specific cell. In contrast, within-subject designs are more resilient: participants provide data across multiple conditions, so dropouts affect the dataset more evenly and often less severely. As a result, between-subject designs require a larger buffer to account for potential attrition, increasing recruitment demands and the risk of compromised statistical validity.

This sample size concern increases significantly as the complexity of the factorial design increases. For instance, a 3×2 factorial design involves three levels of one factor and two levels of another factor, leading to six experimental conditions. As the number of factors and levels increases, so does the number of possible experimental conditions and the complexity of the analysis. Researchers use software tools, such as *R* or *SPSS*, to conduct factorial ANOVA, which can handle large and complex datasets with multiple factors. There is no strict maximum number of factors in a factorial design, but the practical limit is determined by several factors, including the complexity of the experiment, the available resources, and the sample size. As the number of factors increases, the number of experimental conditions grows exponentially. For instance, in a 2-level factorial design, if you have k factors, the total number of conditions is 2^k. So, if you have five factors, the number of conditions will be 32, and for ten factors, the number of conditions will be 1024. This rapid growth can make it impractical to run experiments with a very high number of factors, as the number of conditions could become prohibitively large to source a sample for.

Conceptualizing Exponential Growth

Imagine you're playing a series of poker hands, and each hand can vary based on several factors: the number of players at the table, the betting structure (no-limit, pot-limit, fixed-limit), the position you're sitting in, the type of opponents you face (tight, loose, aggressive), and whether there are any special rules like antes or straddles. Each of these factors doubles or multiplies the number of possible game scenarios you might encounter. So, if you have five such factors, the total combinations of different game situations multiply quickly–leading to dozens or even hundreds of unique hands with different dynamics. This explosion in possible scenarios makes it nearly impossible to prepare for or analyze every situation thoroughly. Just as it would overwhelm a poker player trying to memorize perfect strategies for every possible hand combination, it challenges researchers to design experiments that remain manageable and statistically valid despite the complexity.

However, for such large-scale experiments, between-subjects designs are the optimal choice because participants in the experiment only have to be exposed to one of many conditions. Because exposing a single participant to every condition in a large factorial design would require an impractically long time, within-subject designs risk participant fatigue, dropout, or learning effects that undermine data quality. As a result, researchers often end up treating the study like a between-subject design anyway—dividing conditions across different participants—which increases the total number of subjects needed and complicates the design. By conducting multi-factor experiments through between-subject design, the onus is on the researcher to navigate the increased model complexity, however. As you increase the number of factors, the number of interactions between them increases rapidly. For example, in a 3-factor design, there are not only three main effects (one for each factor), but also three two-way interactions (for each pair of factors), one three-way interaction, and so on. With larger numbers of factors, the model can become very complex, requiring careful consideration of which interactions to include and how to estimate them. In high-dimensional designs, researchers may need to use specialized statistical methods like regularization or dimensionality reduction to deal with the sheer complexity of the model.

In a large factorial experiment, interactions between factors might be significant, but estimating these interactions requires substantial data and might introduce the risk of overfitting. If the model becomes too complex, it could also become harder to interpret, and for others to understand the theoretical motivations. For architects, working with complex notions of space and place, high-dimensional factorial designs make a lot of sense to examine the interaction between different design decisions—so it is up to the researcher to explain these interactions to the reader. If working in higher-order factorial design, you increase the number of comparisons in an experiment, and so the probability of making at least one false positive also increases, because each statistical test comes with its own chance of error. The Benjamini–Hochberg procedure (Appendix D) is often a good choice when controlling for Type I errors in architectural experiments that involve multiple comparisons.

In architecture, there are also specific concerns when experiments involve physical environments. In rooms, buildings, or materials, it is often impossible to control all contextual factors that might influence outcomes. Variables like weather conditions, lighting quality, ambient noise, or even the time of day can vary between groups in a between-subject design, introducing unwanted noise and threatening internal validity. Because each participant experiences only one condition, these contextual differences become confounding factors that can mask or mimic the true effect of the experimental manipulation. Within-subject designs mitigate this issue by exposing the same participant or unit to all conditions, effectively controlling for stable contextual influences. When controlling the physical environment is impractical or impossible, one viable alternative is to use survey or vignette-based experiments. These allow researchers to manipulate and present hypothetical scenarios consistently across participants, eliminating variability from real-world environmental factors while preserving experimental control.

For architects, between-subjects designs are often the only way to test manipulations that are irreversible or conceptually biasing. Consider a major urban design firm preparing a single application for a new public housing community. Success depends not only on the design itself but also on how the proposal is presented, making it critical to identify the most persuasive narrative. The firm can run an experiment prior to submission to test which approach maximizes support. Condition A (Control Narrative) describes the design in plain, technical terms—density, budget, and material performance—while Condition B (Treatment Narrative) presents the same design using aspirational, high-concept language emphasizing "community cohesion," "biophilic connection," and "equitable urban integration."

The dependent variable (Y) is the public's perceived quality and support for the project, measured on a rating scale. If the same participant read both narratives, the second reading would be confounded by the first; they might become hyper-aware of the manipulation or average their opinions. A between-subjects design avoids this problem by assigning each participant to only one condition, providing a clean measure of whether the high-concept narrative alone (Condition B) causally increases public support, even when the underlying design is identical. By empirically demonstrating which presentation strategy is most effective, architects can tailor proposals to maximize the likelihood of winning municipal or federal grants, ensuring that abstract, communicative elements are optimized alongside technical design.

While specific architectural firms are often secretive about the empirical testing of live grant applications—as the winning persuasive language is a key competitive trade secret—the underlying methodology is rigorously employed in adjacent fields. For instance, behavioral economics labs frequently run between-subjects experiments that confirm this exact principle. Their research might test two different narratives describing the same energy-saving technology: one focused on personal financial savings (Condition A) versus one focused on collective environmental duty (Condition B). Because a respondent's preference is highly sensitive to the initial framing, the results are always analyzed via a between-subjects design to prevent the "contamination" of one ethical framework by the other. Architects then operationalize these validated findings, using the research to choose the narrative frame (Savings vs. Duty) that they know will resonate best with the specific municipal board or private client reviewing their proposal. They are testing the rhetorical effectiveness, not the design itself—a critical aspect of architectural work.

To analyze the results, researchers typically use an Analysis of Variance (ANOVA) approach. However, this differs fundamentally from the repeated-measures ANOVA in how it handles variability. In a between-subject ANOVA, because each participant contributes data to only one condition, the total variance includes both between-group differences (the effect of the factors) and between-subject variability (individual differences unrelated to the factors). This individual variability adds to the error term, making it harder to detect true effects and justifying the greater sample size required. Between-subject ANOVA operates under simpler assumptions than within-subject design, largely because each participant contributes data to only one condition, ensuring that observations are independent.

It requires homogeneity of variances and that the outcome variable is approximately normally distributed within groups. This assumption can often be upheld through careful and consistent design of experimental conditions, and by being attentive to conditions that may elicit universally high or low responses. Identifying and addressing these ceiling or floor effects during pilot testing or early analysis can help ensure that group variances remain reasonably comparable. Crucially, between-subject designs do not require assumptions about the covariance structure of repeated measurements, as there are no repeated measures per participant. This independence and lack of within-subject correlation make the model's assumptions less complex and often easier to satisfy compared to within-subject designs.

For a 2x2 between-subject design, the ANOVA model would be represented as:

$$Y_{ijk} = \mu + \alpha_i + \beta_j + (\alpha\beta)_{ij} + \epsilon_{ijk}$$

where

- $i = 1,2$ indexes levels of Factor A (e.g., ceiling height: low, high).
- $j = 1,2$ indexes levels of Factor B (e.g., lighting: ambient, task).
- Y_{ijk} is the outcome variable for participant k in the given condition (i,j).

- μ is the overall mean.
- α_i and β_j are the main effects of the two factors (e.g. ceiling height and lighting type).
- $(\alpha\beta)_{ij}$ is the interaction effect between the two factors.
- ε_{ijk} represents the error term (residual variation in the data that cannot be explained by the model) among participants within the same condition.

In this context, the statistical significance of the main effects and interaction effects is tested using F-tests (Appendix C). If the p-value associated with an effect is <0.05, it suggests that the effect is statistically significant.

Any factorial experiment where a significant main effect involves a factor with three or more levels, such as those appropriate in between-subject designs, requires the use of post hoc tests to determine which specific levels of that factor yield significantly different average outcomes from each other, while simultaneously controlling for the increased risk of Type I errors that arises from conducting multiple comparisons. This is because ANOVA by itself only indicates that there is an overall significant difference somewhere among the average outcomes for the levels of that factor; it does not specify which particular pairs of levels are significantly different from each other. To pinpoint these specific differences while maintaining statistical rigor, researchers commonly employ various post hoc tests, each with its own approach to controlling the family-wise error rate—the probability of making at least one false positive across all the comparisons being performed.

When researchers aim to compare all possible pairs of means for a factor and seek a good balance between controlling the risk of Type I errors and maintaining statistical power, Tukey's Honestly Significant Difference (HSD) is often a preferred choice. This test works by calculating a single "honestly significant difference" value, which is the minimum difference between any two means required for them to be considered statistically significant (Appendix E). By doing so, it effectively controls the family-wise error rate across all pairwise comparisons, ensuring that the overall chance of a false positive remains at the desired level (e.g., 5%).

Conversely, when balancing the discovery of true effects with control over false positives is important, the Benjamini–Hochberg procedure is often preferred. Unlike highly conservative methods that control the chance of any false positive, Benjamini–Hochberg controls the false discovery rate—the expected proportion of false positives among all significant findings. This method adjusts the significance thresholds based on the rank order of the p-values and the total number of comparisons, allowing for a less stringent but more powerful approach. For example, if ten comparisons are made with a desired false discovery rate of 0.05, the threshold for significance varies for each test depending on its rank, often resulting in higher adjusted p-value cutoffs than traditional corrections. While this increases the likelihood of detecting true effects, it still maintains a controlled rate of false discoveries, making it especially useful in studies with many simultaneous tests.

Between-subject experimental design, through its fundamental reliance on distinct, independently exposed groups, provides a uniquely clear lens for assessing human responses to architectural interventions. By ensuring each participant experiences only one specific design condition, this approach effectively safeguards against the confounding biases of memory, learning, or sequential comparison inherent in other designs, thereby yielding purer, untainted reactions. While it necessitates meticulous attention to random assignment for initial group equivalence and often requires larger sample sizes to manage inherent individual variability, the data generated from such experiments offer unparalleled clarity regarding the direct and uninfluenced impact of specific design choices.

Chapter 7
Variable Design: Identifying and Controlling Variables

Chapter Definitions

Confounding Variable

An outside factor that varies along with the independent variable and can influence the dependent variable, making it impossible to tell whether the observed effect is due to the independent variable or the confound.

Example: Investigating whether rough wall textures (IV) enhance perceived coziness (DV) could be confounded by the ambient temperature (confound), as colder rooms might feel less cozy regardless of surface material.

The precise identification, definition, and control of variables are the fundamental building blocks upon which any robust experiment is constructed. Without a clear understanding of what is being manipulated, what is being measured, and what extraneous factors are being held constant, even the most innovative research question remains unanswerable, yielding ambiguous or misleading conclusions. Clarity ensures that the experiment can accurately test the hypotheses it is designed to evaluate, and that the results can be interpreted meaningfully. Indeed, the very power of experimental research lies in its ability to isolate the specific causal impact of one element on another. Achieving this demands not just a keen eye for what can be changed, but a rigorous discipline in anticipating and neutralizing influences that might otherwise obscure genuine effects. For experimentalists seeking to understand the intricate relationship between people and the built environment, this meticulous variable design is paramount. It is the core mechanism through which we transform broad questions about how spaces affect us into precise, testable propositions, allowing us to move beyond mere correlation to establish definitive knowledge about the designs that shape our world.

C. J. Zolan, *Best Practice for Experimental Methods in Architecture*,
https://doi.org/10.1007/978-3-032-15884-0_7

The independent variable (IV), as the factor intentionally manipulated by the researcher, finds its concrete expression through the distinct conditions to which participants are exposed. These conditions represent the specific, operationalized levels or variations of the IV, meticulously designed to create discernible differences within the experimental environment. These conditions can manifest in a variety of forms, each chosen for its ability to isolate the intended manipulation while maintaining ecological relevance. A condition might be presented as:

- Vignettes—a detailed textual description of a situation, design, or scenario
- High-fidelity photographs or rendered images
- Multimedia stimuli, such as video
- Auditory stimuli
- Virtual Reality (VR) environments
- Physical environments or full-scale mock-ups

Regardless of the mode through which the independent variable is expressed, a well-defined IV ensures that the factor being manipulated is clearly understood and consistent across all experimental conditions. An IV must be consistently clear and precise, plausible and realistic, as well as limited in scope. Clarity requires that participants immediately understand what has changed between conditions. In text-based vignettes, this means using precise, concrete language and avoiding ambiguous phrasing or culturally loaded terms that may be interpreted inconsistently. In visual or multimedia formats, clarity involves visual hierarchy: the manipulated element must be clearly perceptible, ideally without needing explanation. For instance, in a rendered image comparing window sizes, the difference should be obvious without labeling or prompting. Plausibility refers to how believable or credible the manipulation is. A video that shows a fantastical or implausible building scenario may fail to engage participants as seriously as one grounded in architectural realism. In vignettes, this means staying within the bounds of real-world constraints (e.g., budgets, materials, user behavior norms) unless deliberately testing the effect of violating those bounds.

Realism, closely related to plausibility, depends on the sensory and contextual fidelity of the condition. High-fidelity renders, photos, and VR environments should reflect accurate lighting, scale, materiality, and occupancy to simulate genuine spatial experience. For vignettes, this means embedding details that evoke lived experience without overwhelming the participant with irrelevant information. Part of this is considering the issue of salience. An IV must be noticeable enough for participants to perceive the manipulation and respond to it, but not so dominant that it becomes unnaturally impactful compared to how the same factor would function in a real-world context. This is a common pitfall: experimentalists, eager to ensure an effect is detected, may overstate the difference between conditions—such as using an absurdly narrow corridor, a comically bright color palette, or a vignette that presents the manipulated feature in an unnaturally overt or isolated way. While these choices make the IV easy to detect, they also produce an artificial effect size, which risks undermining ecological validity. Participants may respond more strongly than they would in situ simply because the manipulation was too obvious or too extreme.

This distorts both the realism and applicability of the findings. IVs must be perceptible but proportionate—detectable without distorting the scenario.

Finally, maintaining a narrow scope of manipulation is essential for preserving internal validity. Only the intended independent variable should vary between conditions; all other features must remain constant to ensure experimental control and a clean, interpretable contrast. Any unintended variation introduces confounds, making it impossible to isolate the true source of any observed effect. These principles are critical: failure to uphold them undermines construct validity, weakens interpretability, and risks drawing conclusions about variables that were never truly isolated.

Once a variable has been identified at the conceptual or theoretical level—such as "spatial openness," "thermal comfort," or "perceived privacy"—the next step is to operationalize it to translate that abstract construct into a measurable and manipulable form within the experiment. This process is not cosmetic; it determines the validity of the entire study. Operationalization requires identifying specific, observable features or design elements that instantiate the construct in a real or simulated context. For instance, if the theoretical variable is "spatial openness," the researcher must decide what design parameters best represent that—such as ceiling height, window area, or visual connectivity. These choices must be justified, preferably drawing on prior literature, design standards, or pilot testing. The operationalized variable then becomes the independent variable in the experiment, implemented through clearly defined and controlled conditions (e.g., a room with 2.4 m vs. 3.2 m ceiling heights, with all else held constant). Poor operationalization—where the link between concept and condition is vague, inconsistent, or culturally dependent—undermines both the internal and construct validity of the experiment. A well-operationalized variable is one where the experimental manipulation meaningfully and specifically reflects the underlying concept, enabling the researcher to make valid inferences about real-world phenomena (Table 7.1).

Effective operationalization means crafting an experience so seamless and convincing that participants don't just observe the manipulation—they feel it. It's not just a technical step; it's an art form. True immersion demands more than accuracy—it requires intuition, restraint, and a deep understanding of how people perceive and respond to space, material, and narrative. A well-operationalized variable doesn't announce itself—it quietly shapes the participant's perception, drawing them into the experimental world just enough to provoke an authentic reaction, without ever revealing the wires behind the illusion. The above examples demonstrate how variables shift from theoretical IV to operational IV to expression via a text-based vignette in experiments. In all examples presented, manipulation checks confirmed that over 99% of participants correctly identified or perceived the intended variation, indicating exceptionally high clarity and effectiveness in operationalization.

For architects designing commercial or institutional spaces, experimental methods require extreme precision in defining both conceptual and operational variables. Consider the abstract construct of Perceived Corporate Trust or Sense of Welcome in a corporate lobby. Conceptually, this quality is intangible, but it can be

Table 7.1 Table showing operationalization of independent variables across conditions

Abdu Resaba (عبده رصابا) is a country in the Middle East with a population of 35m people. The leader, Emir Abdullah al-Thani, controls a repressive dictatorship. Abdu Resaba is rich in energy resources, but the local population has a low level of income, education, and development. Locals are religious and conservative, and the culture is male-dominated.	Veyshnoria (Вейшнория) is a country in the Russian Caucasus with a population of 35m people. The leader, President Vladimir Preobrazhensky, controls a repressive dictatorship. Veyshnoria is rich in energy resources, but the local population has a low level of income, education, and development. Locals are religious and conservative, and the culture is male-dominated.
IV: Middle Eastern Country	*IV: Caucasus Country*
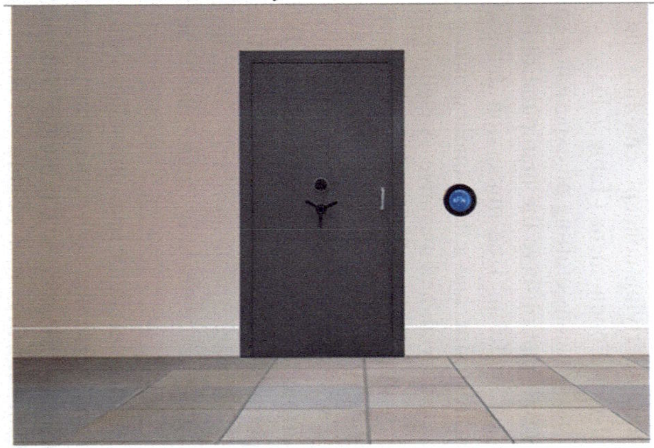	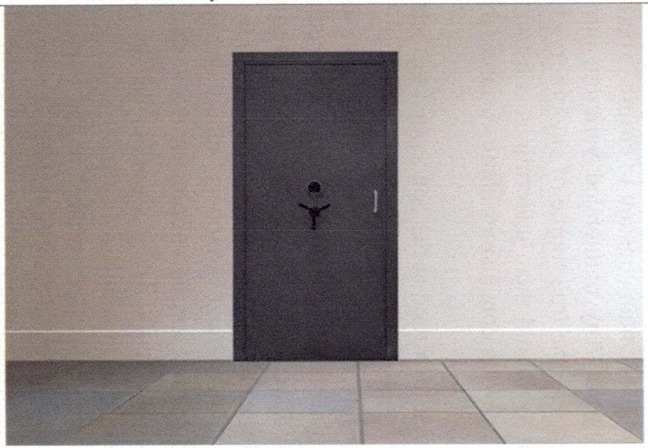
IV: Climate Control (AC/Heat)	*IV: No Climate Control (AC/Heat)*
Shells hit the hospital, resulting in five casualties.	Shells hit the hospital, resulting in 95 casualties.
IVs: Low Casualty Count, No Photo	*IVs: High Casualty Count, No Photo*
In conflict-affected regions, armed groups frequently disrupt children's daily lives by confiscating their belongings and restricting their movement.	Maria, a 12-year-old girl from a small village, was playing outside near a group of insurgents stationed at a checkpoint. They took her skipping rope and teddy bear, shouted at her, and kept her in a room on her own for hours.
IVs: No Personalization, No Detail, Aggregate	*IVs: Personalization, Detail, Individual*

operationalized by varying the medium of information display while keeping the content identical. In one condition, a high-resolution digital screen continuously presents the company's mission statements and abstract visual art. In the other, the exact same messaging and visual motifs are permanently carved into stone or arranged in a mosaic installation, matching color, size, and visual complexity. The only difference between the two conditions is the medium itself—dynamic digital versus static, tactile representation. By carefully controlling all other features of the space, architects can isolate the causal effect of the presentation medium on visitors' perceptions. This approach demonstrates that rigorous operationalization—translating an abstract conceptual variable into a manipulable, measurable design feature—is essential for producing valid, actionable insights in architectural experimentation.

Text-based vignettes are one of the most accessible forms of experimental design, particularly in survey-based research, but their simplicity can be deceptive. Too often, text-based vignettes fall into information overload, ambiguity, and lose the participant. They perform well only when the experimentalist can capture sensory detail, and evoke the experience of the space, engaging senses beyond just sight. Precision in word choice is paramount, ensuring conciseness and economy of language so that every detail contributes directly to the vignette's purpose without overwhelming the reader or introducing unintended cues. The ability to implicitly suggest an atmosphere or spatial quality, rather than explicitly stating it, requires skill in subtle suggestion, allowing participants' own interpretations to emerge from the evoked context. These skills must be deployed equally across all conditions, and that balance takes some practice.

Architects typically think in images, models, and physical or digital spaces, so moving from visual thinking to text requires a deliberate translation process. The first step is identifying the experiential qualities they want to study—light, scale, materiality, circulation, acoustics—then describing them in terms that evoke sensation rather than just naming objects. For example, instead of writing "the corridor is wide," a designer might describe "a corridor that allows two people to walk side by side without brushing shoulders, with sunlight filtering through high windows." The text must carry the same kind of spatial cues and sensory signals that a model or rendering would provide visually. Second, architects must learn to simplify without losing nuance. Unlike visuals, which can show complex relations instantly, text relies on sequencing and word choice to guide the reader's perception. Every sentence becomes a controlled "frame" of the space, just as every view in a drawing or model is curated. This is where training in experimental methods intersects with design skill: thinking about variables, contrasts, and participant interpretation translates the visual design logic into structured, measurable textual forms. Finally, collaboration helps bridge the gap. Practices often bring in research consultants, behavioral scientists, or writers who can shape the architects' observations into testable vignettes, ensuring the descriptions are precise, neutral, and experimentally valid while retaining the richness of the original design intent. Over time, architects develop the skill to convert their spatial intuition into language that can generate reliable participant responses, allowing text-based experiments to stand alongside visual prototypes as tools for evidence-driven design.

Increasingly, architectural firms such as Arup have collaborated with behavioral scientists to test environmental variables through structured text-based experiments, emphasizing "experience design," which integrates cognitive psychology and user interaction early and purposefully in the design process. Architects contribute their expertise in spatial form, materials, and human interaction, which is then translated into precise vignettes or survey descriptions. For example, in early stages of design, before renders are produced, participants might read a scenario describing a busy atrium with a high ceiling, variable acoustic treatments, and staggered pedestrian flows, then report perceptions of comfort, crowding, or noise disturbance. These studies leverage architects' spatial knowledge while producing controlled, measurable experimental data, bridging the gap between design intuition and evidence-based evaluation.

Experiments in architecture uniquely empower architects to showcase their technical and creative skills—whether in rendering, audiovisual production, photography, or virtual reality—by crafting immersive representations of spaces where the designer exercises complete control over every element. As a result, experiments are the most powerful tool to systematically explore how subtle changes in form, materiality, lighting, or spatial arrangement influence human perception and behavior. In designing spaces and experiences for the IV, architects must ensure that these media-based expressions of the independent variable are high-fidelity and contextually accurate: renderings should replicate realistic textures, lighting conditions, and scale; audiovisuals must balance sensory detail without overwhelming participants; VR environments need to offer intuitive navigation and believable spatial cues to maintain immersion. Common mistakes to avoid include over-simplification of spatial features, excessive stylization that distorts realism, inconsistent lighting that confuses visual perception, and poorly calibrated VR interactions that cause disorientation or fatigue. Careful attention to these factors ensures that the manipulated variable is salient but natural, enabling valid inferences about architectural experience without sacrificing ecological or construct validity.

Clear and detailed documentation of independent variable design decisions is paramount for scientific rigor and cumulative progress. Researchers must thoroughly record not only the specific levels or conditions used, but also the precise rationale behind their selection, demonstrating how these choices directly embody the underlying theoretical constructs. Such meticulous transparency empowers other scholars to accurately replicate the experiment, critically assess the manipulation's validity, and build upon the work in future studies. Without this level of detail, the interpretability and long-term scientific value of experimental findings are severely compromised.

Once participants have been exposed to the independent variable through carefully designed conditions, the next step is to collect data on their responses. This typically involves administering measures—such as questions, tasks, or observations—aimed at capturing the dependent variables. Just as precision and clarity are essential in designing the IV, dependent variables must be thoughtfully constructed

Table 7.2 Common operationalizations of theoretical constructs as dependent variables in architectural experiments

Theoretical DV	Operational DV
Wayfinding difficulty	Error count, timer
Spatial openness	Perceived size, with Likert scale room size, ceiling height
User comfort	Self-reported comfort rating, physiological measures
Acoustical comfort	Subjective noise disturbance ratings, perceived decibels
Anxiety	STAI—State-trait anxiety inventory

to accurately reflect the outcomes the study seeks to understand. The chosen outcome should be directly linked to the research question and measurable in a valid and reliable way. In architectural research, dependent variables often include factors like occupants' comfort, mood, productivity, or satisfaction with the space. Below is a table illustrating common ways that theoretical constructs are operationalized as dependent variables in architectural research (Table 7.2).

Crucial to achieving this valid measurement is ensuring content validity, which refers to the extent to which a dependent variable (or any measurement instrument) adequately covers all relevant facets of the theoretical construct it intends to measure, and conversely, does not include irrelevant aspects. It addresses the fundamental question: "Does this measure represent a comprehensive and appropriate sample of the entire domain it's supposed to cover?" For instance, if a study aims to assess "perceived spaciousness," the chosen measure must genuinely encompass all key perceptual elements that contribute to spaciousness, such as ceiling height, depth of view, and density of furnishings, rather than just floor area. If the measure is too narrow or includes unrelated components, the findings about how a design influences spaciousness would be incomplete and potentially misleading. Establishing content validity typically involves a systematic review by subject matter experts to confirm that all critical dimensions of the construct are adequately represented in the chosen dependent variable.

Like independent variables, the DVs must be assessed using standardized, reliable instruments that robustly capture their underlying theoretical construct and align precisely with the study's conceptual dependent variable. Specificity is essential in this process. For example, "comfort" is a multifaceted construct that can encompass thermal comfort, acoustic comfort, visual comfort, or even psychological comfort. A study aiming to understand the effects of lighting design on occupant comfort must clearly define which aspect of comfort is being measured. Simply asking participants, "Are you comfortable?" leaves too much room for interpretation and can introduce noise into the data. If the DV is too narrow or fails to encompass the multiple factors that affect the outcome, the experiment may overlook important influences and fail to fully capture the effects of the independent variable (Lipsey, 1990).

A concrete example of careful dependent-variable selection comes from research by Payedar-Ardakani et al. (2024). In this study, participants experienced nine varying daylight illumination conditions in a virtual-reality office setting and then provided subjective ratings of how pleasant, interesting, calming, or spacious they found the environment—meanwhile, their brain activity was recorded using EEG. The alignment between self-reports and physiological data confirmed that the dependent variable—architectural experience—was meaningfully captured rather than loosely defined. For architects, the takeaway is clear: when you define DVs such as perceived crowding, acoustic comfort, or spatial openness, you must specify exactly how you will measure them and then validate that those measures truly reflect the intended construct. In practice, combining subjective responses with behavioral or physiological indicators strengthens confidence that experimental outcomes correspond to the actual qualities being tested—especially important when converting design conditions into text-based vignettes where clarity and fidelity in the scenario description are critical.

Architects can make in-house experimental measures rigorous by carefully defining the dependent variable, standardizing the conditions under which it is assessed, and triangulating data from multiple sources—without the need to use EEGs. For example, if the DV is perceived spaciousness, it should be operationalized with a specific scale question, a clear context (e.g., a 10-m corridor in VR), and repeated consistently across participants. Observational measures—such as dwell time, navigation errors, or frequency of pauses—can serve as behavioral proxies that validate self-reported responses. Consistency in instructions, timing, and scenario presentation reduces bias, while randomizing variable conditions across participants prevents systematic confounds. Finally, combining quantitative ratings with qualitative feedback (e.g., think-aloud protocols or post-scenario interviews) allows cross-checking; if subjective impressions align with observed behaviors, the measurement can be considered reliable.

The chosen DV should be sensitive enough to detect changes due to the manipulation of the IV but also specific enough to avoid measurement error. It is critical to capture variation, something that binary scales (yes/no) generally fail to achieve. Instead, using well-validated scales that target specific domains ensures the measure aligns closely with the intended construct:

(a) Positive and Negative Affect Schedule (PANAS)

The Positive and Negative Affect Schedule (PANAS) stands as a widely adopted, robust self-report instrument for quantifying distinct dimensions of human emotion: positive affect (capturing feelings like enthusiasm, alertness, and inspiration) and negative affect (encompassing states such as distress, irritability, and nervousness). This questionnaire presents a series of evocative adjectives, where individuals then rate according to their intensity of feeling over a specified period—whether "right now," "today," or "in the past week." This allows experimentalists to specifically assess the period in which the participant was exposed to the condition to increase the validity of the data. An example of this schedule is shown below (Fig. 7.1).

	(1) Very Slightly or not at all	(2) A little	(3) Moderately	(4) Quite a bit	(5) Extremely
1. Interested	☐	☐	☐	☐	☐
2. Distressed	☐	☐	☐	☐	☐
3. Excited	☐	☐	☐	☐	☐
4. Upset	☐	☐	☐	☐	☐
5. Strong	☐	☐	☐	☐	☐
6. Guilty	☐	☐	☐	☐	☐
7. Scared	☐	☐	☐	☐	☐
8. Hostile	☐	☐	☐	☐	☐
9. Enthusiastic	☐	☐	☐	☐	☐
10. Proud	☐	☐	☐	☐	☐
11. Irritable	☐	☐	☐	☐	☐
12. Alert	☐	☐	☐	☐	☐
13. Ashamed	☐	☐	☐	☐	☐
14. Inspired	☐	☐	☐	☐	☐
15. Nervous	☐	☐	☐	☐	☐
16. Determined	☐	☐	☐	☐	☐
17. Attentive	☐	☐	☐	☐	☐
18. Jittery	☐	☐	☐	☐	☐
19. Active	☐	☐	☐	☐	☐
20. Afraid	☐	☐	☐	☐	☐

Fig. 7.1 Example of a PANAS schedule

The strength of the PANAS lies in its concise format, rigorous psychometric foundation, and proven capacity to capture both immediate emotional shifts and more enduring mood patterns. For those investigating the built environment, the PANAS offers a particularly valuable lens for assessing how design interventions—ranging from nuanced changes in light quality or thermal comfort to fundamental shifts in spatial configuration or material palettes—influence occupants' emotional experiences. It proves most effective when the research seeks to precisely measure the affective impact of a space or design element, especially in studies focused on comfort, well-being, or stress responses within architectural contexts.

So, if an architectural firm is evaluating the emotional impact of different lighting strategies in a corporate atrium. Before running the study, the design team reviews the PANAS scale and selects a subset of adjectives most relevant to their design goals—focusing on positive affect terms like "alert," "enthusiastic," and "inspired," and negative affect terms such as "nervous," "distressed," and "irritable." These are chosen to capture how lighting might influence attentiveness, mood, and comfort. Participants experience the atrium in VR under two lighting conditions: one with cool, diffused daylight plus warm accent lighting, and one with neutral overhead lighting only. Immediately following each exposure, participants complete the PANAS questionnaire for that condition, rating the intensity of each selected adjective "right now." The design team then compares positive and negative affect scores across the two lighting scenarios, identifying which lighting combination maximizes positive affect while minimizing negative affect. Observational measures, such as dwell times or circulation patterns, are also recorded to triangulate findings.

By carefully selecting relevant PANAS adjectives a priori and linking the questionnaire directly to specific design conditions, architects can rigorously measure the emotional impact of spatial and material interventions, translating subjective experience into actionable, evidence-based design decisions without requiring advanced physiological equipment.

(b) Continuous Scale

Continuous rating scales offer a method for quantifying subjective experiences along a finer, more granular spectrum. The primary advantage of such scales is their capacity for nuanced understanding, capturing subtle variations in comfort, preference, or sensation that might be overlooked by coarser, binary, or limited-point ordinal scales (Schwarz et al., 1991). For instance, an individual might not simply feel "satisfied" or "dissatisfied" with a space, but can articulate a precise level of satisfaction along a continuous spectrum. The 0–10 scale, in particular, proves superior in experimental testing over a 1–10 scale due to its inclusion of a true zero, allowing participants to indicate a complete absence of the measured quality (e.g., no comfort at all), and providing a natural midpoint (5) for signaling neutrality or ambivalence. An example of this is shown below. This expanded range empowers participants to express subtle differences in their experience, going beyond broad categories (Robinson, 2024) (Fig. 7.2).

This capability is particularly vital in environmental and architectural studies, where the subjective effects of design factors—such as the precise balance of daylighting, the optimal acoustic reverberation in a performance space, or the perceived intimacy versus openness of an interior layout—rarely manifest as simple categories but rather as continuous gradients. For design practitioners and researchers, understanding precisely *when* a space transitions from comfortably illuminated to slightly glaring, or from acceptably quiet to subtly distracting, demands a granularity of data that only continuous scales can provide. They enable the precise mapping of these critical thresholds and subtle experiential shifts, directly informing iterative design refinement and the optimization of human-centered environments. Thus, continuous rating scales become an indispensable tool for accurately quantifying the nuanced and fluid human interaction with the built environment, bridging subjective experience with objective design parameters.

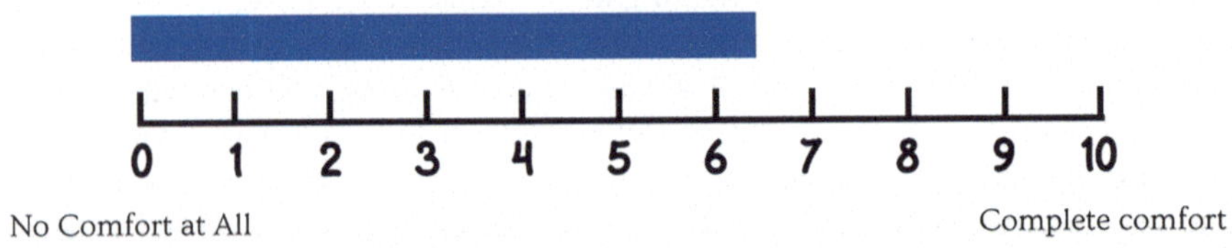

Fig. 7.2 Example of a continuous scale

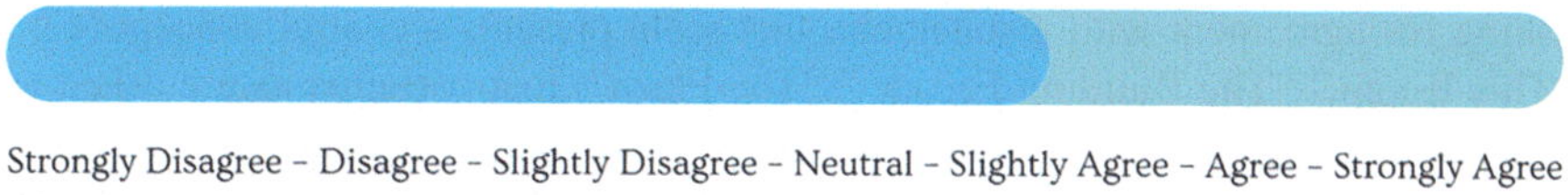

Fig. 7.3 Example of a Likert scale

(c) Likert Scale

The Likert scale helps quantify attitudes, opinions, perceptions, or evaluations along a spectrum of agreement or intensity. Typically presenting a declarative statement or a direct question, it asks individuals to select a response option from a range of ordered choices, such as "Strongly Disagree" to "Strongly Agree," or "Very Dissatisfied" to "Very Satisfied," commonly spanning five or seven points, as shown below (Fig. 7.3).

These formats provide a clear midpoint option for neutrality or ambivalence, while offering enough gradations to capture varying degrees of agreement or feeling without causing respondent fatigue or confusion. Each point on the scale is systematically assigned a numerical value, enabling the transformation of nuanced subjective experiences into quantifiable data suitable for statistical analysis. To ensure the highest quality data when using Likert scales as dependent variables, meticulous attention must be paid to their construction. This includes crafting clear, unambiguous statements that avoid double-barreled questions, and offering balanced response options with psychologically equidistant intervals. The selection of the number of scale points (e.g., 5-point, 7-point) should carefully consider the desired granularity of response and whether a neutral mid-point is appropriate for the construct being measured. Furthermore, clear and consistent labeling of anchor points at both ends and potentially the middle of the scale is crucial for ensuring all respondents interpret the scale uniformly. When meticulously designed and applied, Likert scales provide a robust and widely understood method for quantitatively capturing complex human responses to the built environment.

Architects often discover post-occupancy that visitors get lost or confused in multi-level atria with overlapping paths, visual barriers, or non-orthogonal layouts. To evaluate this early, a design team develops carefully crafted Likert scale statements that directly target participants' perceived navigational clarity, e.g., "The layout of pathways and sightlines helps me understand where I am at all times." The Likert scores quantify subjective navigational experience, allowing comparison across design variations. For example, if participants consistently rate one layout lower on confidence and clarity, this signals a potential circulation problem that might not be obvious in plans or renders. To strengthen rigor, the team can triangulate results with behavioral proxies such as wrong turns, backtracking, or hesitation points. This allows architects to solve a common post-occupancy issue ahead of construction.

(d) Semantic Differential Scales

Semantic differential scales offer a powerful method for quantifying the connotative meaning and subjective qualities of a concept, object, or experience. Rather than asking for agreement with a statement, this scale presents a central concept (e.g., "This Room," "The Building Facade," "The Plaza") that participants are asked to rate across a series of bipolar adjective pairs. Each pair sits at opposite ends of a continuum, often represented by a 5- or 7-point numerical scale between them. In environmental and architectural research, semantic differential scales are exceptionally valuable for mapping complex, often intangible, perceptions of space. They allow researchers to assess how individuals perceive the atmosphere, character, or "feel" of a designed environment along multiple dimensions. For instance, participants might rate a rendered interior on pairs such as "Warm–Cold," "Spacious–Confined," "Modern–Traditional," "Calming–Stimulating," or "Public–Private." This method yields a rich "semantic profile" of the design, providing deep insight into the subjective experiences it evokes.

While both semantic differential and Likert scales utilize a series of numbered points for responses, their fundamental nature differs. A Likert scale measures the degree of agreement or disagreement with a specific declarative statement (e.g., "I agree this space is warm"). The meaning is embedded in the statement itself, and the anchors describe the intensity of your agreement with that statement. In contrast, a semantic differential scale measures the position of a concept on a continuum defined by two opposing attributes. The adjectives themselves are the anchors, defining the bipolar spectrum along which the concept's meaning or perception is placed. This allows for a more direct, intuitive assessment of perceived attributes rather than a reaction to a declarative sentence.

To ensure robust data when employing semantic differential scales, a careful selection of the adjective pairs is critical. These pairs must be truly bipolar, relevant to the architectural context, and psychologically meaningful to the target audience. When thoughtfully constructed, these scales provide a unique and insightful lens for quantitatively exploring the nuanced subjective dimensions of the built environment.

Architects often face subtle challenges in complex urban plazas where multiple activities—cafés, pedestrian flow, outdoor seating, performance areas—intersect. Conventional observation or Likert scales may detect general satisfaction or discomfort, but they struggle to capture nuanced perceptions of spatial character and atmosphere that influence how people feel and behave in space. A semantic differential scale survey focused on the plaza could follow a VR simulation of the plaza under different design conditions—varying paving materials, seating arrangements, shading devices, and visual permeability—and then rate the space along bipolar adjective pairs such as inviting/unwelcoming, flexible/restrictive, and safe/unsafe. This approach lets participants intuitively position the space along continuous, nuanced perceptual axes. This makes it ideal for complex, multi-use environments where the "feel" of the space is more important than any single declarative statement, giving architects actionable insight into subtle but impactful experiential qualities that are otherwise discovered only post-occupancy.

(e) Task Performance

Beyond subjective self-report measures, task performance offers a powerful means to quantify dependent variables through observable, behavioral outcomes. In this approach, participants are engaged in specific activities or simulations designed to reflect real-world functions, with their performance rigorously measured as the dependent variable. This allows researchers to assess the functional impact of varying environmental conditions while the participant is immersed, or was recently immersed, in the vignette (Watson and Clark, 1994). The metrics derived from task performance can be highly diverse and objective. They commonly include measures such as completion time (e.g., how long it takes to solve a complex problem or navigate a virtual building layout), accuracy (e.g., number of errors in a detail-oriented task or correct identifications in a visual search), output quantity (e.g., number of items processed or designs generated per unit of time), or even qualitative aspects of performance (e.g., efficiency of movement patterns, creativity scores for a design challenge).

This method is particularly valuable in architectural and environmental studies because it provides direct, behavioral evidence of how design elements influence human capabilities. The objectivity inherent in these performance metrics offers compelling evidence of the direct influence of the built environment on human productivity, cognition, and interaction, providing critical insights for design optimization. When using task performance as a dependent variable, it is essential to design tasks that are ecologically valid, meaning they realistically reflect the kinds of cognitive or physical activities users would perform in the built environment being studied.

Tasks should be appropriately challenging—neither too easy (which creates ceiling effects) nor too difficult (which introduces frustration or disengagement). Metrics like completion time, error rate, and efficiency must be defined clearly and measured consistently. Researchers should also control for prior experience or baseline skill differences between participants, as these can confound results. Where possible, standardized tasks or pre-calibrated difficulty levels should be used, and pilot testing is crucial to ensure the task functions as intended. Task performance should be interpreted in context: a faster completion time might indicate ease of use, or it might signal a lack of engagement—so pairing performance data with subjective feedback is often essential for meaningful conclusions. Task performance metrics can be coupled with cognitive load measures to determine the mental effort participants expended while interacting with a built environment or completing specific tasks within it, to better navigate this distinction.

Priming an emotion or feeling before a task-based dependent variable is measured can be methodologically useful when the goal is to examine how specific affective states influence performance outcomes. In experiments—particularly those investigating the interaction between spatial environments and cognition or behavior—task performance may be influenced not only by the physical stimulus but also by the participant's psychological state. Priming provides a controlled way to standardize or induce these internal states before task engagement, helping isolate the effect of the manipulated independent variable on performance. For example, if the research question involves how stress-inducing architectural environments affect decision-making or attention, priming participants with a short anxiety-inducing vignette or audio clip ensures a consistent emotional baseline, enabling more accurate attribution of performance differences to the interaction between emotional state and environmental condition.

Priming can be achieved using various stimuli: emotionally charged imagery, brief video clips, evocative narrative vignettes, or even auditory cues like ambient sounds or music. What's critical is that the priming element is subtle enough to avoid obvious demand characteristics but strong enough to reliably activate the intended affective state. In such designs, researchers must also confirm the success of the priming (typically via a brief manipulation check) and ensure the prime does not overwhelm the main IV or DV, maintaining a balance between realism and experimental control.

Acoustic comfort in open-plan offices or multi-use atria is difficult to assess through self-report alone, because occupants often aren't consciously aware of how noise affects their focus or efficiency. Architects can use task performance to measure these effects objectively. Participants are asked to complete a series of cognitive tasks—such as proofreading documents, assembling design diagrams, or solving problem-solving exercises—within a VR or physical simulation of the space under varying acoustic conditions. By systematically varying soundscapes (ambient chatter, overlapping conversations, or background mechanical noise), architects can identify which acoustic conditions degrade task performance and which support focus. Task performance captures the functional impact of design decisions—such as partition placement, material selection, or ceiling treatments—providing actionable evidence for optimizing acoustic comfort.

(f) Visual Analogue Scales (VAS)

This scale is a method of quantifying highly subjective experiences that are inherently continuous, such as pain, fatigue, or the intensity of a perceived sensation. This format typically presents a straight line, usually 100 mm in length, with clearly defined anchors at each extreme representing the full range of the measured construct (e.g., "No discomfort at all" at one end and "Worst possible discomfort" at the other). Participants mark a point on this line that best represents their current experience, and the score is then derived by precisely measuring the distance from one end of the line. The primary strength of a VAS lies in its ability to capture a truly continuous, fine-grained representation of an individual's experience, providing a level of nuance that even multi-point numerical scales might miss. It avoids forcing a participant's complex internal state into predefined categories, allowing for a more accurate reflection of their perception across a fluid spectrum. These are, in the social sciences, often referred to as "feeling thermometers."

To ensure the validity and reliability of VAS data, clear and unambiguous instructions for marking the line are crucial, as is accurate measurement of the mark's position by the researcher. While offering exceptional granularity, the treatment of VAS data in statistical analyses sparks a long-standing debate: whether its scores genuinely possess interval properties (allowing for more powerful parametric tests like *t*-tests and ANOVA) or are strictly ordinal (limiting analyses to non-parametric methods). This contention arises because, while the visual line is continuous, some argue that human subjective perception along this continuum may not truly be linear or equally spaced, thus questioning the mathematical assumptions of interval data.

Nevertheless, due to its proven practical utility, sensitivity, and strong empirical correlations with objective measures, it is widely accepted in applied research to treat VAS data as interval-level for most analytical purposes, provided other statistical assumptions are met.

Architects designing high-end interiors often debate between surface finishes—polished stone, brushed metal, textured wood—but quantifying how tactile these materials are perceived, particularly at a subconscious level, is challenging. Participants explore a space and indicate their experience on a VAS anchored with terms such as "Not engaging at all" to "Extremely engaging" or "Not comfortable at all" to "Extremely comfortable" for walls, flooring, or handrails. This approach captures subtle gradations in material perception, enabling architects to refine surface selection to maximize sensory richness without relying solely on subjective descriptors. The continuous granularity of the scale is especially valuable: small differences in perception, which may appear negligible individually, accumulate across a space, ultimately shaping the overall tactile and experiential quality.

While some experimental designs employ ranking scales, which ask participants to order a set of options based on a specific criterion (e.g., preference, importance, effectiveness), this response format generally possesses significant limitations that make it largely inappropriate for robust causal inference work. The primary drawback stems from ranking data's inherently ordinal nature: it reveals relative order (e.g., A is preferred over B) but provides no information about the magnitude of the difference between ranks. This absence of equal intervals between scale points violates the fundamental assumptions of most powerful parametric statistical methods (like *t*-tests or ANOVA), which are typically used to quantify precise causal effects, effect sizes, and mean differences by assuming measurable distances between data points. Without knowing the actual psychological distance between ranked items, it becomes impossible to determine if an independent variable caused a truly meaningful, measurable shift in outcome or merely altered a relative position. An exception to this limitation arises when the dependent variable itself is explicitly about relative preference or order of choice rather than a measurable intensity; in such instances, the causal inference pertains to what drives that specific ordering. For these situations, researchers must employ non-parametric statistical methods, which do not assume interval data and instead rely on the ranks or frequencies of observations (e.g., Friedman's ANOVA or Mann–Whitney U test), allowing for valid analyses of relational data without inferring magnitudes.

To preserve the integrity of the manipulation and avoid contamination, DVs should typically be collected immediately after exposure to the independent variable condition—before participants have time to reflect, guess the purpose of the study, or be influenced by external factors. When measuring multiple outcomes, randomizing the order of DV questions across participants helps mitigate order effects, where responses to earlier questions influence later ones through priming or response fatigue. However, randomization should be avoided when a logical or temporal sequence is essential (e.g., emotion before behavior). In studies that involve repeated exposure to conditions (such as in within-subject designs), DV data should be gathered after each condition block to prevent retrospective bias.

Conceptualizing Contamination

In poker, the decisions made immediately after the cards are revealed–whether it be the initial deal or the flop–most accurately reflect a player's assessment of the statistical value of their hand. In this moment, the decision is driven predominantly by the objective information presented: card strength, table position, and pot odds. However, as time passes, this clarity can become diluted. The longer a player waits to act, the more likely external and non-statistical factors–such as table talk, perceived tells, or internal doubt–begin to influence their judgment. Similarly, when players are required to make a series of consecutive decisions without sufficient variation or pause, cognitive fatigue may further erode the precision of their reasoning. Thus, early decisions offer the clearest insight into a player's untainted reaction to the hand, while delayed decisions risk being shaped by noise rather than the original signal.

To maintain data quality, researchers must implement strategies that reduce both missing and invalid responses without compromising the integrity of the data. This begins with clear, concise wording, consistent formatting, and intuitive survey or task design that minimizes confusion and participant error. Pilot testing is essential to identify where participants may misinterpret instructions or disengage. While it may be tempting to force responses by making questions mandatory to avoid missing data, this approach often leads to rushed, fabricated, or careless answers that silently degrade the dataset. Offering a "prefer not to answer" option may seem a softer alternative, but it can unintentionally encourage disengagement by signaling an easy out, resulting in data that appears valid but lacks substance. A better approach is to allow participants to skip questions entirely; missing data is visible, manageable, and can be addressed through transparent statistical methods, whereas low-quality responses are hidden and corrosive. Researchers can further safeguard data integrity by incorporating soft validations (e.g., reminders before skipping) and monitoring indicators like completion time or straight-lining.

Variable design is the capstone of impactful architectural experimentation. It's in the careful crafting of independent variables—whether through a subtly altered rendering or a fully immersive VR environment—that we precisely isolate the design elements under scrutiny. And it's in the sensitive measurement of dependent variables—from the nuanced shifts in mood captured by a continuous scale to the objective precision of a task performance metric—that research can come to truly understand human response to the built environment.

References

Lipsey, Mark W. *Design sensitivity*. Newbury Park, CA: Sage, 1990.

Payedar-Ardakani, Pegah, Yousef Gorji-Mahlabani, Abdolhamid Ghanbaran, and Reza Ebrahimpour. 2024. "The Impact of Changes in Daylight Illuminance Levels on Architectural Experiences in Office Environments Using Virtual Reality and Electroencephalogram." *Journal of Building Engineering* 110487. doi:https://doi.org/10.1016/j.jobe.2024.110487.

Robinson, John. "Likert scale." In *Encyclopedia of quality of life and well-being research*, pp. 3917–3918. Cham: Springer International Publishing, 2024.

Schwarz, Norbert, Bärbel Knäuper, Hans-J. Hippler, Elisabeth Noelle-Neumann, and Leslie Clark. "Rating scales numeric values may change the meaning of scale labels." *Public opinion quarterly* 55, no. 4 (1991): 570–582.

Watson, David, and Lee Anna Clark. "The PANAS-X: Manual for the positive and negative affect schedule-expanded form." *Unpublished manuscript, University of Iowa* (1994).

Chapter 8
Robustness Checks: Validating Your Findings

In architecture, the impact of design decisions—spatial layouts, material choices, lighting schemes—on human experience is complex and often subtle. Experimental methods provide architects with evidence-based tools to validate these effects; however, the credibility of the findings depends on robustness checks—procedures that ensure results are not merely artifacts of chance, participant variability, or specific measurement choices. Robustness checks allow architectural teams, whether in-house, in collaboration with behavioral scientists, or through academic partnerships, to rigorously evaluate design hypotheses before committing to costly construction, renovation, or material selections.

Robustness checks are crucial for bolstering internal validity, which confirms that observed changes in the dependent variable are a direct consequence of the independent variable's manipulation, rather than extraneous factors or biases (Lu and White, 2014). The primary goal of internal validity is to ascertain whether the changes observed in the dependent variable are a direct consequence of the manipulation of the independent variable, rather than due to other external factors or biases. These checks are necessary to account for any extraneous influences that might distort the interpretation of the experiment's outcomes. In practice, robustness checks are designed to identify and control for any potential threats to internal validity, such as confounding variables, measurement biases, or participant-related issues like fatigue or demand characteristics.

Consider, for instance, an experiment testing the impact of lighting conditions on mood in an architectural space. A key robustness check might involve examining whether participants' baseline mood influences their responses to the lighting. Without accounting for baseline mood, any observed changes could be mistakenly attributed to lighting when they actually reflect pre-existing emotional states. However, directly measuring baseline mood immediately before the experiment poses a challenge because it can prime participants—making them more aware of their feelings and potentially altering their natural responses. To circumvent this, researchers often assess mood separately from the experimental session, perhaps

C. J. Zolan, *Best Practice for Experimental Methods in Architecture*,
https://doi.org/10.1007/978-3-032-15884-0_8

administering validated scales like the Positive and Negative Affect Schedule (PANAS) several hours or even a day in advance. This temporal separation preserves the authenticity of participants' emotional states during the experiment and allows baseline mood to be statistically controlled in the analysis, strengthening causal inferences. Alternatively, indirect measures or neutral questions that don't explicitly reference mood can infer baseline affect without priming. Another strategy involves using mood data from pilot studies to balance participant mood across experimental groups through stratified randomization, minimizing confounds without measuring mood in the main experiment.

When pre-assessment isn't feasible, post-experiment analyses exploring correlations between mood-related variables and outcomes offer a secondary, though less ideal, robustness check. In designing an office with variable daylight access, an architect could run a robustness check by simulating different window configurations in VR and measuring participants' mood and alertness both before and after exposure. By controlling for baseline mood, the design team can confidently identify which daylighting strategies genuinely improve occupant well-being, rather than reflecting pre-existing differences in mood. This allows the architects to iterate layouts and shading strategies in-house or collaborate with cognitive scientists to validate findings before construction. The overarching principle is to separate baseline measurement from the experimental manipulation itself to avoid priming effects while still accounting for individual differences that could confound results. Beyond simply controlling for obvious confounds, a truly robust finding demonstrates stability even when assumptions or minor methodological choices are varied.

One powerful method for enhancing robustness involves introducing multiple dependent variables that measure different, yet related, aspects of the phenomenon under investigation. This approach provides convergent evidence: if the independent variable produces consistent effects across several distinct measures of the same underlying construct, confidence in the findings increases significantly, indicating that the observed effects aren't an artifact of a single, narrow measure. For example, in an experiment measuring the impact of an architectural space's design on productivity, researchers might use both self-reported productivity (a subjective measure) and task completion time (an objective measure) to capture the full range of potential effects. If both measures show similar patterns in response to the design changes, the evidence for the design's causal impact on productivity becomes much stronger. For example, a co-working space design might use both subjective measures of collaboration (Likert scales) and objective task performance (group problem-solving in VR) to test furniture layouts and circulation. If both measures converge, architects gain stronger evidence that specific arrangements enhance interaction. Consulting behavioral scientists ensures the measures are valid and reliable, while in-house designers can adapt layouts in real time based on early experimental results. This multi-method approach validates the construct being measured from different angles.

Crucially, in the initial design of the experiment, researchers must include attention checks and manipulation checks, which both serve as fundamental safeguards. Attention checks are often simple questions or tasks embedded within the study to verify that participants were fully engaged and accurately perceived the experimental conditions (Abbey and Meloy, 2017). For instance, participants might be asked to recall specific details about a room's design they just viewed or to select a particular response to demonstrate they're reading instructions carefully (e.g., "Please select 'Strongly Agree' to show you're paying attention"). The primary purpose here is to identify participants who may be disengaged, distracted, or otherwise not processing the stimuli as intended. If participants fail these checks, their data are often excluded from the final analysis to protect data integrity. This exclusion process must be clearly documented in the methods section, specifying what counts as a failure and the criteria used for removal. Reporting the number of excluded participants upfront in the results section further demonstrates the rigor and transparency of the experimental approach, safeguarding internal validity and building confidence that findings are grounded in genuine engagement.

Following attention checks, manipulation checks are vital to confirm the success of the independent variable's implementation. These are specific measures, often direct questions or brief assessments that gauge whether participants noticed and were affected by the IV. For example, in an architectural experiment manipulating lighting temperature, a manipulation check might ask participants to rate the warmth or coolness of the lighting they experienced. These checks don't assess the experiment's outcome but validate that the experimental conditions created the intended psychological or perceptual state. Including them helps identify participants for whom the manipulation was ineffective—perhaps due to distractions, technical issues, or individual differences—allowing researchers to exclude or analyze these cases separately. Furthermore, manipulation checks provide direct evidence supporting internal validity, showing that the independent variable was operationalized successfully. Without this confirmation, any null or unexpected results in the dependent variables might stem from a failure to properly deliver the IV rather than from a genuine absence of effect. It's crucial to design manipulation check questions carefully so they directly correspond to the key features of the IV without inadvertently revealing the study's hypotheses or priming participants. Typically, manipulation checks are placed immediately after the experimental condition and before the main dependent variable measures, ensuring they reflect immediate perception. However, in some complex or prolonged experiments, they may appear at the end to assess sustained impact.

Beyond these immediate checks, sensitivity analyses offer robust validation by examining how results vary under different assumptions or conditions (Kleijnen, 1997). At its core, a sensitivity analysis explores the stability and reliability of findings by systematically varying elements of the analytical process. This can include, but isn't limited to, excluding outliers or influential cases, applying different statistical models or parameter settings, adjusting for alternative operationalizations of variables, or modifying data handling strategies such as the treatment of missing values or imputation methods. The objective is to identify whether the main conclusions hold consistently across these different analytical decisions or whether they shift significantly, indicating potential fragility.

Sensitivity analyses encompass a variety of techniques. Case exclusion or influence analysis systematically removes outliers, influential data points, or participants who failed attention or manipulation checks. This is particularly valuable in between-subject designs where individual variability can disproportionately affect group means, allowing researchers to assess how sensitive findings are to extreme or potentially problematic cases. Model specification sensitivity involves testing how results change when alternative statistical models or assumptions are employed. For example, in factorial designs, researchers might compare fixed-effects ANOVA results with mixed-effects models that account for random participant or item effects, especially crucial when standard model assumptions are questionable in complex architectural experiments involving nested data structures. Operationalization sensitivity assesses whether different ways of measuring a construct influence the results; for instance, comparing findings when subjective comfort is measured via Likert scales versus continuous rating scales. This is particularly relevant in within-subject designs where subtle variations in measurement can impact detected effects.

Data handling sensitivity examines the impact of decisions about missing data treatment, such as using listwise deletion versus multiple imputation, ensuring findings aren't unduly biased by data processing choices, particularly in longitudinal or repeated-measures designs. Lastly, time or sequence sensitivity checks are critical in within-subject designs, where participants experience multiple conditions over time. Researchers might analyze whether order effects or fatigue bias findings by comparing analyses including versus excluding later trial data or by statistically controlling for presentation order. Including these analytical approaches strengthens the internal validity of the experiment and increases the confidence that the observed results are truly reflective of the underlying relationship being tested, making the findings more credible and impactful for informing architectural design practice.

Robustness is a fundamental mindset—a commitment to designing experiments as rigorously as they design buildings. Just as a structure's integrity depends on anticipating stresses and selecting materials from the ground up, a robust experiment is conceived with potential confounds, participant variability, and measurement nuances in mind, even before a single participant is recruited. The strategies are integral components of the initial experimental blueprint and the analytical strategy. They compel the architect-researcher to consider not just what is being manipulated and what is being measured, but how the human experience might genuinely unfold and what extraneous factors could obscure that truth.

References

Abbey, James D., and Margaret G. Meloy. "Attention by design: Using attention checks to detect inattentive respondents and improve data quality." *Journal of Operations Management* 53 (2017): 63–70.

Kleijnen, Jack PC. "Sensitivity analysis and related analyses: a review of some statistical techniques." *Journal of Statistical Computation and Simulation* 57, no. 1–4 (1997): 111–142.

Lu, Xun, and Halbert White. "Robustness checks and robustness tests in applied economics." *Journal of Econometrics* 178 (2014): 194–206.

Chapter 9
Virtual Reality in Architectural Experiments

Imagine designing a building and being able to walk through it, feel its spatial qualities, and even test how its subtle details affect human perception and behavior—all before laying a single brick. For generations, architects have grappled with the inherent challenge of studying the complex, often intangible, human experience of space outside of costly physical mock-ups or messy, uncontrolled real-world environments. How do you precisely isolate the impact of a specific ceiling height, a particular material texture, or a nuanced lighting condition on mood, productivity, or wayfinding, when countless other variables are always at play? Virtual Reality (VR) offers an unprecedented bridge between the controlled precision of the laboratory and the rich, sensory experience of real space. VR isn't just about viewing a digital model; it's about inhabiting it, creating a compelling sense of "being there" that transcends traditional representations. It's uniquely suited to architectural experimentation because it grants researchers absolute dominion over every environmental parameter—from precise dimensions and light quality to ambient sounds—while simultaneously immersing participants in a highly realistic and believable architectural experience.

At the most accessible end of the spectrum, one might encounter experiences akin to a video walkthrough viewed without a headset or a Google Maps Street View type of immersion. While these offer panoramic or navigable digital content, they fundamentally lack the key elements that define true VR: stereoscopic vision (providing depth perception), head-tracking (where the view changes accurately with head movement), and the crucial sense of presence. Without a dedicated headset, the user remains firmly anchored in their physical environment, observing a screen rather than feeling truly enveloped by the virtual space. This diluted experience significantly limits their physiological and psychological responses, diminishing the realism crucial for robust architectural studies.

Dedicated VR systems generally fall into two categories: tethered headsets and standalone headsets, plus specialized large-scale setups. Tethered headsets connect to powerful external computers via cables, offering superior graphics and

C. J. Zolan, *Best Practice for Experimental Methods in Architecture*,
https://doi.org/10.1007/978-3-032-15884-0_9

processing for detailed models and complex simulations with minimal latency. This makes them ideal when precise visual detail matters. Their drawbacks include the need for expensive hardware, restricted movement due to cables, complex setup, and potential participant fatigue from headset weight and tethering. Standalone headsets are all-in-one devices with built-in processors and batteries, requiring no external computer or cables. They're easier to deploy, more portable, and cost-effective, allowing greater participant freedom and comfort. However, their graphics and processing capabilities are lower, which can limit realism for highly detailed models or advanced lighting, and data transfer often requires extra steps.

Beyond individual headsets, CAVE (Cave Automatic Virtual Environment) systems represent the pinnacle of immersive VR in architectural research. These room--sized installations project virtual environments onto multiple walls, immersing participants without requiring them to wear a headset (though stereoscopic glasses are often needed). CAVE systems offer unparalleled fidelity for multiple users and facilitate natural body movement and group collaboration within the simulated space. They virtually eliminate motion sickness common with HMDs for some users and offer an intuitive, large-scale experience. Their limitations are substantial: astronomical cost, requiring dedicated physical space, and highly specialized technical expertise for setup, calibration, and content creation. Data integration can be complex due to the multi-projector, multi-sensor setup. They are typically found only in well-funded research institutions.

A critical consideration for any VR architectural experiment, particularly those seeking to scale up or conduct remote studies, is the cost and accessibility of the hardware. While standalone headsets have made VR more affordable (typically \$500–\$1000 for a capable headset), this still represents a significant investment for an individual. This inherent cost creates a stark limitation for participant pools in remote experiments, effectively restricting participation to a specific demographic that already owns or can afford such equipment. This likely skews towards a younger, more tech-savvy, and potentially higher-income demographic, raising concerns about the generalizability of findings beyond this niche group. Researchers must weigh the benefits of remote deployment against the potential for biased or unrepresentative samples.

Looking ahead, emerging trends in VR promise to further refine architectural experimentation. Eye-tracking integration within headsets allows researchers to precisely measure a participant's gaze, revealing where attention is directed within a virtual space—a crucial metric for understanding visual perception and wayfinding in architectural contexts. Haptic feedback devices, ranging from controller vibrations to specialized gloves, offer the potential to simulate the tactile experience of materials (e.g., the roughness of a concrete wall, the smoothness of glass), adding another layer of sensory realism. The growing integration of mixed reality (MR), which overlays virtual elements onto the real world (or vice-versa), holds promise for studies examining the interaction between designed virtual elements and an existing physical context. All these advancements, however, necessitate robust hardware/software compatibility with common experimental platforms and analysis tools, requiring ongoing technical development and adaptation for widespread research utility. The trade-offs between cost, accessibility, and the fidelity afforded by these emerging technologies will continue to shape the frontier of VR in architectural research.

The power of virtual reality in architectural research stems from its capacity to immerse participants, yet this very immersion presents a series of deliberate choices that dictate the validity and generalizability of the findings. The core challenge lies in the inherent tension between achieving high fidelity—how closely the virtual environment replicates reality—and maintaining rigorous experimental control—the ability to precisely manipulate specific variables while holding all others constant. One of the foremost principles in creating experimental VR spaces is understanding this fidelity vs. experimental control trade-off. Achieving absolute photorealism can be incredibly resource-intensive and, paradoxically, might introduce subtle, uncontrolled details that act as confounds, inadvertently influencing participant responses. Conversely, a highly schematic or abstract virtual space, while offering maximum control over manipulated variables, may lack the ecological validity necessary for participants to respond genuinely. The goal is to strike a delicate balance: achieving sufficient realism to evoke authentic spatial perception and behavior, without sacrificing the precision needed to isolate the independent variable. For instance, a study investigating the psychological impact of ceiling height might prioritize accurate scale and lighting over hyper-realistic material textures if textures are not the primary variable of interest. The chosen level of photorealism versus schematic representation must always serve the specific research question and the intended manipulation. The stills below in Fig. 9.1 illustrate the level of realism achievable in VR experiments, shown from the participant's point of view inside the headset.

Lighting, for example, is a powerful architectural variable that can be manipulated with exquisite precision in VR. Researchers can systematically alter light temperature, intensity, directionality, or the presence of natural light (e.g., sun angles, sky conditions). Textures must be applied with scale accuracy and proper tiling to avoid distracting visual artifacts; a texture that appears realistic up close might look repetitive or distorted from a distance, undermining immersion. Spatial acoustics, often overlooked, can be meticulously designed in VR to simulate reverberation, sound occlusion, or the presence of specific sound sources (e.g., distant city hum, office chatter). This allows for experimental manipulation of acoustic comfort or perceived privacy. Maintaining scale accuracy throughout the virtual environment is non-negotiable; even slight distortions in proportions can profoundly alter perceived spaciousness, comfort, or legibility. Using standardized units and cross-referencing against real-world dimensions during the modeling process is critical.

A key advantage of VR for architectural experimentation is the ability to use modular designs to systematically manipulate specific architectural variables. Instead of building entirely new environments for each condition, researchers can design a base module and then swap out components. For instance, to manipulate room dimensions, a base model of an office can be altered by simply adjusting wall positions to create conditions of varying length, width, or height, while keeping all other elements (furniture, objects, lighting fixtures) constant. Similarly, material

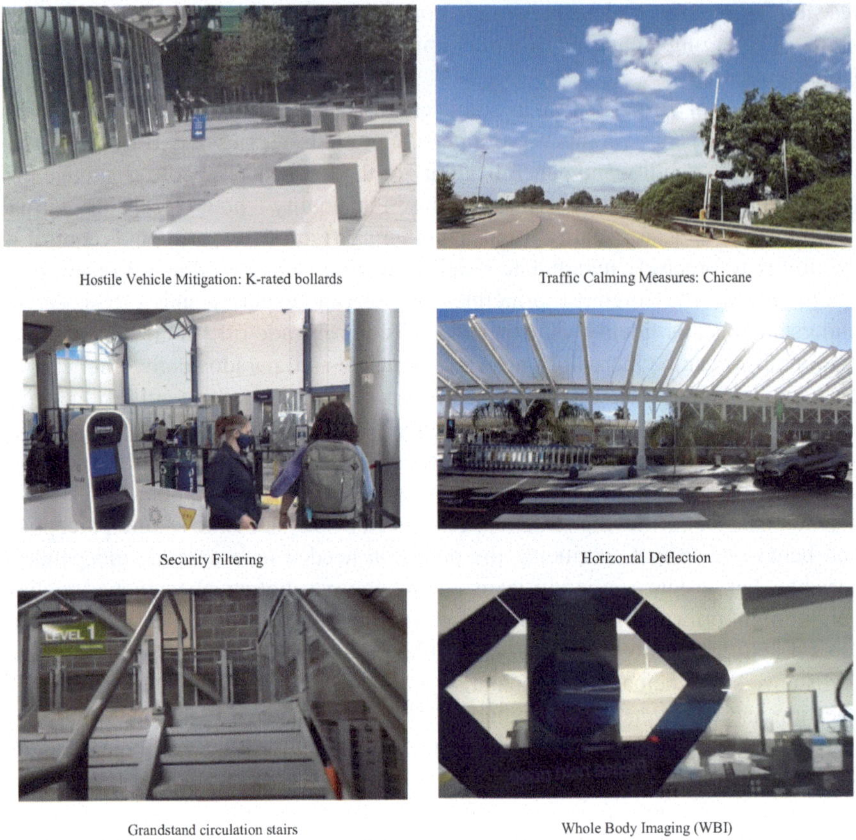

Fig. 9.1 Examples of realism in VR experiments

finishes can be manipulated by assigning different texture maps (e.g., wood vs. concrete floor, matte vs. glossy wall paint) to the same surfaces across conditions. The presence or absence of windows and their size or placement can be precisely controlled, as can the density or type of furnishings. This modularity ensures a high degree of experimental control and facilitates efficient iteration of experimental conditions.

Managing participant navigation and interaction is crucial to standardize exposure to the manipulated variables and collect reliable data. This often involves designing the experimental procedure to ensure all participants experience the virtual environment in a consistent manner. Researchers might implement a guided walkthrough, where participants are prompted to move to specific viewpoints or interact with certain elements in a predefined sequence. Alternatively, free exploration can be allowed, but with recording features that track participant movement paths, gaze patterns (with eye-tracking), and interaction points to ensure sufficient exposure to the manipulated areas. Simple, intuitive navigation controls (e.g., teleportation, smooth locomotion via a joystick) should be prioritized to minimize cognitive load and potential simulator sickness, ensuring that participant discomfort doesn't confound the results related to the architectural variables themselves. The goal is always to create a seamless, controlled, yet naturalistic experience that isolates the intended architectural manipulations and elicits authentic human responses.

Within the controlled realm of virtual reality, architectural experiments gain significant advantages in bolstering internal validity, largely by mitigating confounding factors that plague real-world studies. In a physical environment, variables like fluctuating weather conditions, unpredictable ambient noise, or dynamic uncontrolled lighting (e.g., passing clouds, changing sun angles) can inadvertently influence participant responses, obscuring the true effect of the intended architectural manipulation. VR, however, grants the researcher absolute dominion over these elements. The virtual sky can maintain a consistent brightness and cloud cover across all participants and conditions; background sounds can be precisely controlled or eliminated; and lighting—be it natural or artificial—can be rendered with unvarying intensity, color temperature, and directionality. This unprecedented ability to eliminate or precisely standardize extraneous variables ensures that any observed changes in dependent variables are far more likely to be a direct consequence of the manipulated architectural elements, significantly strengthening causal inferences. Furthermore, VR allows for meticulous control over participant movement, viewpoint, and interaction, ensuring consistent exposure to the independent variable. Unlike navigating a physical building where individual exploration varies widely, VR environments can employ guided walkthroughs, restricted movement zones, or automated camera paths to guarantee that every participant experiences the manipulated architectural features (e.g., a specific corridor width, a distinct material palette) from the same angles and for the same duration. This standardization of exposure is vital for minimizing within-group variance and maximizing the interpretability of observed effects.

Virtual reality uniquely enables the seamless integration of attention checks by leveraging the rich behavioral data it inherently captures—without adding extra burden on participants. Modern VR headsets often include built-in gaze tracking, which provides precise, objective information about where participants direct their attention, how long they fixate on specific architectural elements such as windows or furnishings, and their overall visual exploration patterns. This allows researchers to verify whether participants are truly attending to key features of the virtual environment, serving as a powerful, unobtrusive attention check. Additionally, VR automatically records movement metrics—such as walking speed, navigational paths, and time spent in different zones—which can reveal whether participants are engaging fully with the space or merely moving through it superficially. Interaction logs capture every action taken, from button presses to object manipulations, offering further evidence of active engagement. By embedding these objective attention checks directly into the VR experience, researchers can confidently ensure participant attentiveness without disrupting the flow of the experiment, thus enhancing data quality and internal validity.

While VR offers unprecedented control for architectural experiments, its unique characteristics also introduce ethical considerations. Given highly granular and sensitive data are collected, there are heightened data security and privacy concerns. Researchers must implement stringent protocols for anonymization, secure storage, and limited access to prevent unauthorized use or breaches of this deeply personal information. Realistic expectations are crucial here: while VR offers unparalleled control in lab settings for specific architectural variables, scaling experiments to broader field deployments inevitably confronts these biases and logistical complexities. Researchers must proactively address these challenges, acknowledging the inherent limitations while strategically leveraging VR's unique strengths to advance architectural knowledge.

Chapter 10
Pilot Testing: Why It Matters

Pilot testing is a strongly recommended, even vital, step in the experimental design process. It serves as a crucial trial run to test the practicality, clarity, and functionality of your experimental setup, ensuring that your intended stimuli and measurements operate exactly as expected. In architecture-based research, pilot testing provides an invaluable opportunity to refine experimental conditions, verify the effectiveness of measurement tools, and preemptively address any issues that could compromise the quality of the data collected during the full-scale experiment (Fraser et al., 2018).

One of the first critical aspects to evaluate during the pilot test is the clarity of the experimental instructions and stimuli. For example, if participants are exposed to different room designs or lighting conditions, it is paramount to ensure that the images or descriptions of these spaces are unambiguous and clearly understood. Any confusion about the experimental conditions can introduce unnecessary variability or measurement error, thus participants should ideally grasp the manipulation without needing extra explanation. Beyond clarity, pilot testing also helps assess whether the experimental stimuli are engaging enough to maintain participant attention throughout the study and whether the conditions remain consistent across all trials.

Another key consideration is the effectiveness and feasibility of the measurement tools themselves. Any survey or questionnaire used to collect responses should be thoroughly tested for clarity and reliability. Are the questions truly capturing the intended constructs, such as mood, comfort, or satisfaction? Can participants easily navigate the survey and respond to questions in a logical, straightforward manner? If the measurement involves more complex instruments—like physiological sensors to measure heart rate or skin conductance—pilot testing is essential to ensure these devices function correctly without introducing technical difficulties. Moreover, pilot testing provides a chance to gauge the overall timing of the experiment. An experiment that is too long risks participant fatigue or disengagement, especially in architecture-related studies involving physical spaces or virtual simulations, which

C. J. Zolan, *Best Practice for Experimental Methods in Architecture*,
https://doi.org/10.1007/978-3-032-15884-0_10

can significantly affect the quality of responses. Testing the duration in the pilot phase helps ensure participants aren't overwhelmed or bored, which could undermine the internal validity of the study (Guo et al., 2016). Similarly, the order in which conditions are presented should be tested to ensure no fatigue or carryover effects distort the results. Generally, a sweet spot of around 15 min, maximum, is often ideal for participant engagement, unless the stimuli are exceptionally interesting or there's significant compensation.

A critical part of pilot testing is also evaluating the logistical feasibility of the entire study. This includes assessing whether the necessary resources for conducting the experiment are sufficient and manageable within the constraints of time, space, and equipment, especially if it involves setting up physical spaces or simulations. While general pilot testing principles apply universally, the unique characteristics of Virtual Reality (VR), Augmented Reality (AR), and other immersive environments introduce specialized considerations that extend beyond ensuring comfortable timing or mitigating physical hazards. For architectural experiments leveraging these technologies, rigorous piloting of the technical aspects is paramount to guarantee data validity and a consistent participant experience, preventing the technology itself from becoming a confounding variable.

A primary focus in piloting immersive environments is the technical stability and effectiveness of the VR/AR system itself. Researchers must meticulously test aspects such as tracking accuracy for head, hand, or body movements. Any jitter, drift, or latency in tracking can immediately break a participant's sense of presence, induce motion sickness, or lead to inaccurate behavioral data as users struggle with unresponsive controls or disorienting visual cues. Similarly, the rendering quality and consistent frame rate must be rigorously assessed. Low frame rates, inconsistent visual fidelity, or graphical glitches can severely impact immersion, cause discomfort, and fundamentally alter a participant's perception of the simulated architectural space, thus compromising the very stimuli under investigation.

Beyond individual components, the overall immersion quality needs careful evaluation during piloting. This includes assessing how convincingly the virtual environment creates a sense of "presence" —the feeling of truly being in the simulated space. Factors contributing to this, like spatial audio, realistic lighting, accurate scale, and appropriate level of detail, should be tested for their consistency and impact on participant experience. Pilot participants can provide invaluable qualitative feedback on where the "illusion" breaks down or where the technical aspects detract from their engagement with the architectural design. Ensuring seamless transitions, stable network connectivity (for multi-user experiences), and robust error handling are also crucial to prevent experiment crashes or unexpected behaviors that could lead to data loss or participant frustration. Ultimately, piloting immersive environments is about verifying that the technology serves as a transparent and reliable medium for the experimental design, rather than becoming an unintended variable itself.

Furthermore, pilot testing offers an opportunity to assess the practicality of randomization procedures, such as the random assignment of participants to different conditions, ensuring the process works smoothly and does not introduce unexpected biases. An effective pilot test is typically run with a small, yet representative, subset of the target population. This approach allows researchers to gain insights from participants who closely resemble those in the full-scale study without expending excessive resources. Often, recruiting between five and ten participants is sufficient for identifying major design flaws or ambiguities. Crucially, pilot testing isn't just about observing task completion; it's about understanding the participant's experience and thought process. Researchers should employ methods designed to elicit rich qualitative feedback, such as "thinking aloud" protocols, where participants verbally articulate their thoughts, perceptions, and any confusion as they navigate the experiment. Post-test semi-structured interviews are also invaluable for probing specific aspects of the design, questions, or environmental conditions that might have been unclear or frustrating. Observing non-verbal cues, task completion times, and error patterns also provides critical data for assessing the user experience within the experimental setup. The pilot phase should always be viewed as an iterative process: initial findings may lead to significant revisions, and if substantial changes are made to the methodology, instructions, or instrumentation, it is often wise to conduct a second (or even third) smaller pilot test to ensure the revisions have effectively addressed the identified issues and haven't inadvertently introduced new problems.

Architects face unique challenges when pilot testing design-related experiments that extend beyond typical laboratory constraints. Physical space setups may be costly or time-consuming to construct for pilot runs, limiting the number of conditions or spatial variations that can be tested. VR or AR simulations, while more flexible, introduce technical issues such as hardware variability, user discomfort, or motion sickness that can confound results. Participant interpretation can also vary widely—architectural designs often rely on subtle cues like scale, proportion, or materiality that may not be fully perceived or appreciated in a pilot, especially by non-expert participants. To mitigate these limitations rigorously, architects can adopt multi-tiered strategies: conducting small-scale mock-ups or modular prototypes to test specific spatial elements, using controlled VR environments for repeated trials across conditions, and combining qualitative "thinking aloud" protocols with quantitative measures to capture discrepancies in participant perception. Stratifying pilot participants by familiarity with architecture or relevant environmental experience can also reveal whether certain cues are universally perceived or require designer explanation. By systematically documenting and addressing these challenges, architects ensure that pilot testing not only identifies superficial procedural issues but also rigorously validates whether the stimuli truly convey the intended experiential qualities.

While undeniably beneficial, pilot testing comes with its own set of common pitfalls that researchers must actively avoid. One significant trap is conducting a pilot with too small or unrepresentative a sample, which can lead to missing crucial issues or drawing incorrect conclusions about the study's viability. Another common mistake is failing to adequately analyze the pilot data, treating the pilot merely as a rehearsal rather than a vital data collection phase for refinement. Researchers might also make too many changes after the pilot test without truly understanding the root cause of issues, or, conversely, make too few changes out of reluctance. Perhaps the most detrimental pitfall is treating pilot data as part of the main study data; pilot data is for refinement, not for inclusion in final analyses, as it comes from a different version of the experiment. Proper documentation of all changes made during the pilot phase is essential to ensure transparency and replicability.

After the pilot test, the researcher must carefully review all feedback from participants and meticulously assess the collected data. Any issues that were identified—whether in the clarity of instructions, the quality of the measurement tools, the overall feasibility of the experiment, or the participant experience—should be thoroughly addressed before launching the full-scale study. Adjustments can range from refining survey questions and modifying experimental conditions to reorganizing the schedule or altering recruitment strategies to better balance the demands placed on participants. It's through this rigorous post-pilot review and subsequent refinement that a robust methodology is truly forged.

Ultimately, pilot testing is not just a recommended step; it's an indispensable investment in the quality, validity, and efficiency of experimental research in architecture. By diligently identifying and resolving potential issues before main data collection begins, researchers can preempt costly errors, enhance participant experience, and significantly boost the reliability and impact of their findings, ensuring that their contributions to the built environment rest on the firmest possible methodological ground.

References

Fraser, Joy, Dorothy Willy Fahlman, Jane Arscott, and Isabelle Guillot. "Pilot testing for feasibility in a study of student retention and attrition in online undergraduate programs." *The International Review of Research in Open and Distributed Learning* 19, no. 1 (2018).

Guo, Yimeng, Jacek A. Kopec, Jolanda Cibere, Linda C. Li, and Charles H. Goldsmith. "Population survey features and response rates: a randomized experiment." *American Journal of Public Health* 106, no. 8 (2016): 1422–1426.

Chapter 11
Ethics and the IRB: Ensuring Ethical Research Practices

When conducting experimental research in architecture, adhering to ethical guidelines and obtaining approval from an Institutional Review Board (IRB) are fundamental steps in ensuring the protection of participants and the integrity of the research process. The IRB is an independent committee that evaluates the ethical aspects of research studies involving human participants. Its primary role is to ensure that research complies with ethical standards and regulations designed to protect the rights, welfare, and safety of participants. This process is especially important in architectural research, where the stimuli could involve physical spaces, virtual environments, or even behavioral observations that may influence participants' emotions, perceptions, and well-being.

The modern framework for ethical human subjects' research is largely rooted in foundational documents like the Belmont Report, which articulates three core ethical principles that guide all ethically sound research: Respect for Persons, Beneficence, and Justice. Respect for Persons emphasizes the importance of treating individuals as autonomous agents, capable of making informed decisions about participation, and calls for protecting those with diminished autonomy. Beneficence compels researchers to maximize potential benefits to participants and society while meticulously minimizing potential harms. Justice dictates that the burdens and benefits of research are distributed fairly across different populations, ensuring that no group is exploited or unfairly excluded from the opportunity to benefit from research advances. These principles serve as the bedrock upon which the IRB's comprehensive review process is built, guiding decisions related to informed consent, meticulous risk assessment, and equitable participant selection.

The IRB review process begins with the researcher submitting a detailed protocol outlining the research design, including a description of the study's objectives, methodology, and potential risks (Yanow and Schwartz-Shea, 2016). The protocol should explain the specific experimental conditions participants will be exposed to, such as different architectural designs, environmental factors, or virtual simulations. This includes providing information on the type of data that will be collected, how

C. J. Zolan, *Best Practice for Experimental Methods in Architecture*,
https://doi.org/10.1007/978-3-032-15884-0_11

it will be used, and the procedures for ensuring confidentiality and data security. Researchers must clearly explain how they will minimize any potential risks to participants, including physical, psychological, or emotional harm that could arise from exposure to particular environmental conditions or research activities. For example, if participants are asked to experience a room design that might provoke discomfort or anxiety, the researcher must provide adequate safeguards and ensure that participants are fully informed of what to expect. In addition to minimizing risks, the IRB will assess whether the benefits of the research outweigh any potential harm to participants. This is an important ethical consideration, particularly when dealing with architectural environments that might have lasting effects on participants' perceptions of space or the built environment. The IRB may require researchers to include steps that ensure participants are not unduly influenced by the research context. For instance, it may recommend that researchers include debriefing sessions to explain the purpose of the experiment, dispel any misconceptions, and ensure participants are emotionally or psychologically unaffected by their involvement.

Participant consent is another key element that the IRB scrutinizes. In experimental research, obtaining informed consent is essential. Participants must be fully aware of the nature of the study, the conditions they will experience, and the potential risks involved. This consent must be voluntary, and participants should be given the option to withdraw from the study at any time without penalty. Researchers are also required to ensure that the language used in consent forms is clear, accessible, and free from technical jargon that might confuse participants. In some cases, researchers may use a written consent form; while in other studies, verbal consent may be sufficient (Tai, 2012). In either case, the process must be transparent and ensure that participants' rights are protected throughout the study. The IRB also evaluates how researchers will handle sensitive data, particularly in studies where personal information might be collected. For example, if participants are asked about their emotional responses to different architectural designs, researchers must ensure that all personal data is anonymized or pseudonymized to protect privacy. Data security measures must be robust, and participants must be informed about how long their data will be retained and how it will be disposed of after the study's completion. Researchers should also disclose whether any third parties will have access to the data and the extent of that access.

Once the IRB approves the research protocol, the researcher is required to adhere to ethical guidelines throughout the study. This includes continuous monitoring of participant well-being, ensuring that no adverse effects occur during the study, and providing clear channels for participants to report any issues or concerns they may have. If the research deviates from the approved protocol at any point, the researcher must seek re-approval from the IRB before proceeding. The IRB's role does not end with approval; researchers often must submit periodic reports to ensure that the study continues to comply with ethical standards. Additionally, if any unanticipated risks or ethical issues arise during the study, the IRB must be notified, and corrective actions should be taken immediately. Ethical conduct in experimental research in architecture not only ensures that participants are treated with respect and care but also helps to maintain the credibility and trustworthiness of the research process. By undergoing rigorous ethical review and following the appropriate procedures, researchers can ensure that their findings are not only scientifically sound but also ethically responsible, fostering a positive relationship between research and the public.

The rapid advancement of virtual reality (VR), augmented reality (AR), and other immersive technologies has opened unprecedented avenues for experimental research in architecture. Researchers can now simulate environments with high fidelity, offering controlled and repeatable conditions that might be impractical or impossible in physical spaces. However, this profound capability introduces a novel layer of ethical considerations that extend beyond traditional experimental paradigms. The immersive nature of these environments means that participants are not merely observing a stimulus; they are often experiencing a profound sense of "presence" within a digital world, which can elicit powerful and sometimes unexpected responses.

The high level of immersion can lead to feelings of disorientation, motion sickness, or even anxiety, particularly if the simulated environment is complex, claustrophobic, or designed to evoke specific emotional responses (e.g., studies on stress in dense urban settings). In cases where simulations depict sensitive or potentially distressing scenarios (e.g., disaster preparedness simulations), there is a risk of inducing trauma or blurring the lines between simulated and real experiences, especially for vulnerable individuals. Prolonged VR use can also lead to visual fatigue, eye strain, or motion sickness that persists after the experience, so limiting the length of the experiment is critical. In room-scale VR setups, participants might inadvertently collide with physical objects in the real world or trip over cables if not properly supervised or guided, necessitating clear safety protocols and adequate supervision.

The nature of data collection and privacy also takes on new dimensions in immersive environments. Beyond traditional survey responses, VR/AR platforms can capture a vast array of passive behavioral and physiological data, often without explicit participant input. This can include precise head and body movements, gaze patterns (eye-tracking), physiological responses (e.g., heart rate if biometric sensors are integrated), and even vocalizations. While invaluable for research, the collection of such highly granular and potentially identifiable data raises significant privacy concerns. Researchers must clearly articulate what data will be collected, how it will be used, stored, anonymized, or de-identified, and for how long.

Given these complexities, the process of informed consent becomes even more critical and nuanced. Participants must fully comprehend the unique nature of an immersive experience, including potential sensory discomforts, the extent of their immersion, and the specific types of behavioral or physiological data being passively collected. Consent forms should use clear, accessible language to describe these aspects, perhaps even including a brief "try-before-you-buy" introductory phase to allow participants to gauge their comfort level with immersion before committing to the full experiment. It is also worth considering the inclusion of a debriefing, in these more immersive experimental designs. Researchers may explain the study's full purpose, address any potential misconceptions, and check for lingering psychological or physical effects. Providing participants with an opportunity to discuss their experience, ask questions, and offer feedback can be useful in mitigating any potential harm and ensuring participant well-being. For particularly impactful or potentially distressing simulations, researchers should also be prepared to offer resources or referrals for support if needed. It is precisely this pursuit of authentic and uninfluenced responses, particularly in complex or subtle experimental manipulations, that sometimes brings researchers to consider the delicate balance between full transparency and the methodological necessity of withholding certain information, leading to a deeper examination of deception in research.

While informed consent is a cornerstone of ethical research, a challenging ethical dilemma arises when the full disclosure of a study's purpose or methodology could inadvertently bias participants' responses, thereby compromising the scientific validity of the findings. This leads to the nuanced consideration of deception in research, which involves intentionally misleading participants or withholding certain information about the true nature of the study. Deception can generally be categorized as active deception, where false information is directly provided, or passive deception (or concealment), where certain details are simply withheld. It is crucial to distinguish between forms of deception that pose significant ethical concerns and those that are often considered methodologically essential for the integrity of the data collected. The types of deception that IRBs are most concerned about are those that could cause significant physical or psychological harm, involve substantial misrepresentation of risks, or fundamentally compromise a participant's ability to provide truly informed consent about their major involvement or any potential dangers. Such practices are generally deemed unethical and are rarely, if ever, approved.

In contrast, "essential deception" primarily refers to the use of passive deception, where specific hypotheses or the precise mechanic being investigated are concealed. This is particularly relevant in architectural and behavioral research aiming to understand genuine, spontaneous human reactions that would be impossible to observe if participants knew the full research agenda. For instance, if a study aims to understand unconscious emotional responses to specific spatial proportions, explicitly telling participants, "We are testing if you feel more comfortable in a golden-ratio room," would almost certainly trigger demand characteristics—where participants alter their behavior to conform to what they believe is the researcher's hypothesis. This would lead to biased and invalid data, rendering the entire research effort meaningless. In such cases, the true variable of interest might be subtly embedded or concealed within a broader, plausible cover story to ensure the authenticity of responses and protect the scientific integrity of the findings. This form of concealment is not intended to harm or exploit participants, but rather to obtain data that genuinely reflects human experience free from the influence of preconceived notions about the study's aim.

When a research question is such that it cannot be effectively answered without the use of essential deception and provided the researcher can demonstrate to the IRB that the study offers substantive benefits and that the deception conceals no information vital to a participant's informed willingness (such as significant risks or deeply personal topics), then this type of design becomes a necessary and ethically justifiable approach for experimentalists to protect the integrity of their findings. Where concerns arise, debriefing serves as the antidote to deception where participants can be fully informed about the true purpose of the study, any deception that was used, and the reasons why it was necessary. However, where concerns arise about participants interacting post-experiment prior to the completion of overall data collection—such as in online surveys or crowdsourced experiments where participants might discuss live studies on forums or social media—researchers may need to strategically delay full debriefing. This delay is crucial for preventing participants from revealing the experimental "mechanic" or deception to subsequent participants, thereby safeguarding the integrity of the data and avoiding contamination from demand characteristics.

Another major challenge in navigating IRB procedures emerges when conducting international or cross-cultural research. As architectural, engineering, and construction problems grow increasingly global—ranging from the design of climate-resilient infrastructure across diverse environments to evaluating user experiences in culturally distinct urban contexts—experimental designs rooted in a single domestic framework quickly reveal their limitations. IRBs place significant limitations on the ability to conduct this type of research, particularly due to concerns around export control regulations and the requirement for foreign ethical approvals.

In many countries, conducting research involving human subjects—even remotely—can theoretically require approval from a local ethics board. However, when the study is conducted entirely online and outside the framework of a local institution, there is often no appropriate or accessible IRB in the target country to evaluate the research. This creates a paradox: the home institution's IRB may demand evidence of local ethical approval, but no such mechanism exists, especially in countries without centralized or formal IRB infrastructure for non-affiliated foreign researchers. Even simple survey-based studies targeting international participants can be stalled by this gap, despite posing minimal risk. The result is a bureaucratic impasse that disproportionately hinders cross-cultural and global experimentation in architectural and engineering research.

Additionally, U.S.-based researchers must comply with federal export control laws—such as the International Traffic in Arms Regulations (ITAR) and the Export Administration Regulations (EAR)—which restrict the transfer of certain technologies, data, or research outputs to foreign nationals or institutions. While these laws are critical for protecting national security and controlling sensitive technologies, their application to academic research is often overcautious and inconsistently interpreted by institutional IRBs and compliance offices. In fields like architecture and engineering, where the experimental data may involve materials, systems, or software with potential dual-use implications, IRBs may take a blanket approach and deny or heavily restrict international components of a study, even when the actual research poses minimal or no risk under export regulations. This is often a misapplication of the law: the majority of basic academic research—especially when published openly and not subject to access controls—is explicitly exempt from export control under the "fundamental research" exclusion. Nevertheless, institutional risk-aversion can create barriers that stall or shut down otherwise compliant and low-risk global research collaborations, particularly in experimental design fields that increasingly demand international perspective.

The ramifications of these procedural impasses are not merely academic; they can have profound real-world consequences. A poignant example arose from an experiment that explored how to design safe rooms that people are willing to enter and remain in, using a VR mockup with varying furnishing designs. Intended for Reddit's r/Israel (a US-based online platform), this study experienced repeated delays and multiple revision requests based around the implied international nature of the study. During this protracted period, lives were tragically lost when individuals failed to enter or prematurely exited shelters, underscoring the urgent real-world cost of prolonged ethical review processes as the below graph shows (Fig. 11.1).

Criticism of the U.S.-centric nature of experimental research is common, and often justified, particularly when findings are generalized across diverse cultural or environmental contexts without appropriate international data. However, what is less often acknowledged is the structural barrier created by institutional policies that actively prevent researchers from conducting international or cross-cultural studies. Overly rigid interpretations of export control laws, the impractical demand for foreign IRB approvals in online or independent research, and the general risk-aversion of institutional review boards make global experimentation difficult, if not impossible, to carry out ethically and legally within institutional boundaries. As a result, researchers may default to U.S.-based samples—not out of methodological laziness, but because institutional systems make international research prohibitively difficult to implement. This creates a self-reinforcing cycle: the absence of global data feeds the perception of academic parochialism, while the institutional structures that could support broader engagement remain inflexible and unexamined.

That is not to suggest that all burdens on international research are unreasonable; many are both legitimate and essential to uphold. It is inappropriate to simply repeat a study identically internationally without careful consideration of local customs, social hierarchies, communication norms, and traditional knowledge systems. This deep cultural understanding is not merely an ethical nicety; it is crucial for methodological rigor and ensuring the high quality and validity of research outcomes. Without it, researchers risk formulating culturally irrelevant or even offensive research questions, designing data collection instruments that elicit biased or superficial responses, or misinterpreting observed behaviors and spatial perceptions through an ethnocentric lens. For example, a direct question about personal comfort designed for a Western context might be considered impolite or yield socially desirable but inaccurate answers in a collectivist culture. Similarly, certain architectural elements or virtual stimuli might carry vastly different symbolic meanings or emotional valences across cultures, leading to flawed interpretations if not understood within their local context.

In cross-cultural experimental research, accurately conveying the meaning of survey questions, experimental instructions, consent forms, and stimuli is paramount. A common yet critical mistake is to rely solely on word-for-word, literal

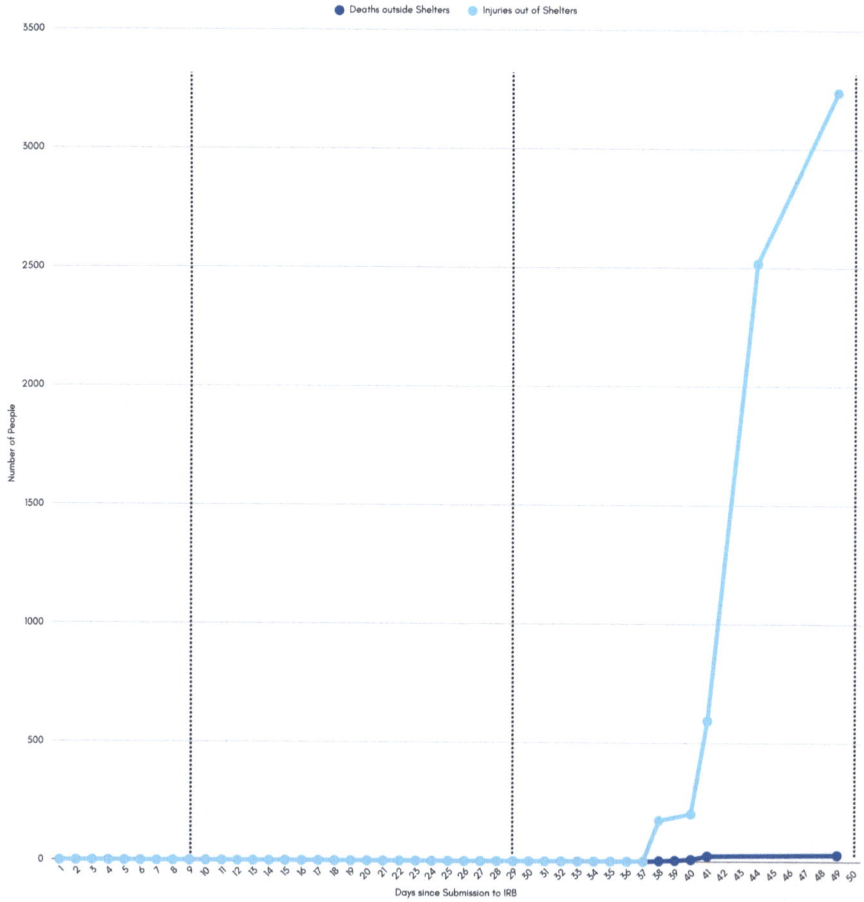

Fig. 11.1 IRB processing timeline for experimental submission on safe room design in Israel, plotted against daily civilian casualties from shelter non-use during warning periods. Dotted lines indicate IRB intervention points (e.g., export control or national origin inquiries)

translations, which often fail to capture the nuanced meaning, idioms, or cultural context inherent in the original language. This can lead to semantic inaccuracies, misinterpretation by participants, and ultimately, low-quality or invalid data that cannot be reliably compared across different cultural groups. The goal should always be to achieve conceptual equivalence—ensuring that the concepts and meanings conveyed are understood in the same way by participants across all language versions, even if the literal words differ.

To achieve this, the gold standard in cross-cultural research is often a double-blind translation process, typically involving a technique known as back-translation with reconciliation. This rigorous method begins with an independent translator, fluent in both the source and target languages and ideally familiar with the research context, translating the original research materials (e.g., questionnaire, script) into the target language. Following this, a second independent translator, also fluent in both languages, translates the newly created target language version back into the original source language. Crucially, this second translator is "blind" to the original source text; they only see the forward-translated version. This "blind" step is vital as it helps reveal ambiguities or misinterpretations introduced during the initial translation.

The final stage involves the meticulous comparison of the original source text, the forward translation, and the back-translation, typically by the research team and/or an expert panel. Discrepancies, ambiguities, or areas where meaning has been lost or altered are identified and then resolved. This expert panel often includes native speakers of both languages, subject matter experts, and professional translators, who engage in iterative discussion and refinement to ensure the wording in the target language best preserves the original conceptual meaning and cultural appropriateness, sometimes requiring multiple rounds of revision until a high level of conceptual equivalence is achieved. This rigorous, multi-step process ensures that research instruments, instructions, and even descriptions of architectural stimuli are understood as intended by all participants, regardless of their linguistic background. While time-consuming and resource-intensive, investing in high-quality double-blind translations is an ethical and methodological imperative. It safeguards the validity and reliability of cross-cultural data, allowing for meaningful comparisons and preventing the generation of misleading findings that could otherwise result from linguistic and conceptual disparities.

Notably, a significant limitation lies in balancing experimental rigor with ecological validity. Architects must ensure that adjustments made after a pilot do not over-optimize the experience for a small subset of participants, which could reduce the generalizability of findings. Mitigation strategies include using pilot feedback to inform but not dictate design modifications, conducting multiple, staggered pilot tests across diverse participant groups, and maintaining a clear distinction between technical/clarity issues and fundamental design variables. Additionally, documenting all changes, their rationales, and any residual uncertainties helps preserve transparency and allows subsequent researchers or collaborators to interpret results in context. In practice, these measures enable architects to refine experimental procedures while retaining confidence that their findings reflect genuine human responses to the built environment rather than artifacts of pilot-specific conditions.

Ultimately, ethical conduct in experimental architectural research isn't a mere compliance exercise; it's the bedrock of credible and impactful inquiry. Experiments are never conducted in isolation; rather, they establish precedents and set the tone for future experimentalists. As a result, upholding ethical integrity ensures that the pursuit of knowledge about the built environment not only advances the field but genuinely serves the well-being and trust of all participants. This commitment also lays the groundwork for future research, fostering greater engagement and enhancing the quality and quantity of participation in subsequent experiments.

References

Yanow, Dvora, and Peregrine Schwartz-Shea. "Encountering your IRB 2.0: what political scientists need to know." *PS: Political Science & Politics* 49, no. 2 (2016): 277–286.
Tai, Michael Cheng-Tek. "Deception and informed consent in social, behavioral, and educational research (SBER)." *Tzu Chi Medical Journal* 24, no. 4 (2012): 218–222.

Chapter 12
Experimental Processes: From Setup to Launch

Creating the actual experiment is the next step. Experiments are ordinarily deployed via survey, and there are many platforms that can be used to achieve this. Qualtrics, one of the most widely used survey platforms in academic and commercial research, offers an extensive range of features that support both basic and advanced survey design needs. Researchers can use Qualtrics to create surveys that present different architectural stimuli, such as photographs of spaces, videos, or interactive virtual environments. Qualtrics' robust randomization features allow for the random assignment of participants to different conditions or the randomization of question in order to minimize biases and control for order effects. Researchers can also set up branching logic, which tailors the survey path based on participant responses. For example, if a participant rates a particular room design highly, the survey could automatically present a set of follow-up questions related to their preferences for lighting or furniture layout. Qualtrics also provides tools for survey timing and response validation, which are critical in experimental research. Researchers can set time limits for specific sections or the entire survey, ensuring that participants don't rush through the experiment. For instance, if the experiment includes a task where participants are exposed to various architectural designs, researchers can track the time spent on each design to analyze how long exposure to certain spaces affects responses. Additionally, response validation tools help ensure that participants answer questions in a way that aligns with the intended format (e.g., numeric answers within a defined range), reducing data entry errors and improving the quality of the responses.

Architects conducting experiments face unique challenges when deploying stimuli that reflect real-world spaces. High-fidelity images, videos, or interactive VR environments often require significant technical resources, and minor inconsistencies—such as lighting variations, image resolution, or navigation controls in VR—can introduce confounds. To mitigate these risks, it is advisable to standardize stimuli across participants, pre-test display hardware, and ensure software performance is consistent. When physical spaces are used, logistical constraints such as

C. J. Zolan, *Best Practice for Experimental Methods in Architecture*, https://doi.org/10.1007/978-3-032-15884-0_12

furniture availability, room scheduling, or seasonal lighting changes can affect experimental control; staggered testing, replication across multiple sessions, and careful documentation of environmental conditions can help maintain internal validity.

Another key feature of Qualtrics is its ability to handle complex question types, such as Likert scales, semantic differential scales, and sliders, which are often used to assess participant attitudes, satisfaction, or comfort in architectural experiments. The platform's powerful analytics tools allow researchers to analyze survey responses in real time, offering data visualization options like bar charts, histograms, and heat maps, which are especially useful when interpreting complex data sets related to space perception or user experience. For example, after participants complete a survey about their perceptions of a particular office design, the results can be easily segmented by demographic characteristics, like age or job role, providing deeper insights into how different groups respond to the design. There are many cost-effective solutions too, and many more emerging since Qualtrics ended its research license. Notable inclusions are GuidedTrack, Survicate, HSDMetrics, Lime Survey, and ngSurvey.

These platforms also assist with randomization. Achieving this in experimental design is critical to ensuring that the results are valid and generalizable. Randomization helps minimize bias, control for confounding variables, and ensures that each participant has an equal chance of being exposed to the different conditions. This process allows researchers to attribute differences in the DV to the manipulation of the IV, rather than to extraneous factors. Most survey design tools, like Qualtrics, have the option to introduce randomization of participants into a condition, as well as randomization of the order of questions. It is important to remember that randomization of the questionnaire following exposure to stimuli should only occur after the main dependent variable is measured because randomizing the order of questions after participants have been exposed to the stimuli could introduce bias or confusion that impacts the measurement of the DV. If questions related to the dependent variable (e.g., perception of space, comfort, mood) are randomized before participants have had a chance to fully process the stimuli, their responses may be influenced by the order or context in which they are asked, rather than by their genuine perceptions or behaviors. This could distort the findings and undermine the validity of the experiment.

For example, if the first question after exposure to a space asks about overall comfort, followed by more specific questions about lighting, layout, or acoustics, participants may begin to form an overall opinion of comfort before evaluating the individual aspects of the environment. The sequence in which questions are asked can influence how participants process and respond, making it crucial to ensure that the DV is measured in a clear, consistent, and unbiased way before introducing any randomization in the order of follow-up questions. Therefore, while randomizing certain elements of the survey can improve the robustness of your experimental design, it's important to maintain a logical flow of questions. Questions directly related to the DV should be measured first, followed by questions that examine other variables or aspects of the study, such as additional perceptions, emotional responses, or specific environmental features. This approach helps maintain the integrity of the DV measurement and ensures that randomization does not confound the results.

Presenting only one question per page when measuring dependent variables is a best practice in experimental survey design, especially in studies aiming for high internal validity. This approach minimizes cognitive load, reduces the risk of participants skipping questions or answering carelessly, and prevents earlier questions from unintentionally influencing responses to later ones. When multiple questions are shown simultaneously, participants may scan ahead, backtrack, or infer relationships between items that were not intended, introducing unwanted biases or demand characteristics. Online experiments, particularly those simulating architectural experiences, are prone to distractions, multitasking, or rapid, inattentive responses. Embedding attention checks and incorporating interactive elements, such as sliding scales or brief manipulation exercises, can help verify engagement. Combining these with qualitative "think aloud" or post-survey feedback allows researchers to detect confusion or misinterpretation of stimuli, ensuring the data accurately reflects participants' experiences. Displaying one item at a time helps to preserve the psychological isolation of each measure, ensuring that each response more accurately reflects the participant's unprimed reaction to the independent variable. It also supports more precise response timing data, which can serve as a useful auxiliary measure in behavioral studies. Especially in architectural experiments where subtle environmental changes are being evaluated, this level of control is essential for preserving the clarity and interpretability of the results.

There are several strategies for recruiting participants, depending on the research goals, resources, and timeline. One of the most common approaches is to use online recruitment platforms, such as Amazon Mechanical Turk (MTurk), Prolific, or social media channels. These platforms provide access to a wide pool of participants with diverse backgrounds, making it possible to gather data from different demographic groups. MTurk, for example, is popular in academic research because it offers a cost-effective way to recruit participants for a range of experiments, from simple surveys to more complex tasks. Prolific is another option that ensures a more demographically balanced sample, as it allows researchers to filter participants based on specific characteristics, such as age, location, or education level. MTurk samples, while hotly debated, have been found to be representative of the US population (Aguinis et al., 2021; Cheung et al., 2017).

Social media platforms, such as Facebook, Instagram, or Twitter, can also be effective for recruiting participants, particularly if you are conducting a study related to a specific demographic group or geographic location. For example, you might use targeted Facebook ads to recruit participants who are likely to have experience with certain types of architectural spaces, such as office workers for a study on workplace design. LinkedIn can be a useful platform for recruiting participants in professional fields or for studies related to the workplace environment. It is also possible to recruit participants from specific organizations or communities. This could include approaching local universities, architecture firms, or housing associations, where participants may already have some relevant experience or interest in architectural design. In these cases, the researcher may be able to recruit participants directly, either by sending invitations via email or through flyers posted in common areas. This method is particularly useful when the study requires a specific type of participant, such as those working in a certain industry or those who have experience with certain types of spaces. These two methods tend to result in reduced external validity, an issue discussed later.

Incentives can play a significant role in motivating participants to take part in a study, especially in online environments where participants are typically compensated for their time. Monetary rewards, such as small payments or gift cards, are commonly used to encourage participation in survey-based experiments. Other incentives, such as entries into prize drawings or donations to charitable causes, may also be effective depending on the target audience. When offering incentives, it's important to balance the value of the reward with the level of effort required from participants, ensuring that the incentive is appealing enough to drive participation but not so large that it creates an ethical conflict or leads to biased responses (Voslinsky and Azar, 2021). Overly generous incentives may introduce coercion or draw participants primarily motivated by compensation, while insufficient incentives risk disengagement or careless responding. Incentives can also inadvertently shape the dependent variable itself—particularly in studies measuring subjective constructs like satisfaction, motivation, or comfort—by introducing extraneous motivation unrelated to the experimental manipulation. Furthermore, the promise of a reward can activate demand characteristics, where participants alter their behavior to align with perceived expectations. These risks are compounded when using online panels, which tend to overrepresent experienced survey-takers accustomed to maximizing earnings.

Participant variability poses additional challenges. Architectural perception is often influenced by prior spatial experience, cultural background, or professional expertise, which can introduce noise into the data. Stratifying samples based on relevant experience, pre-screening for key demographic or professional characteristics, and statistically controlling for these factors during analysis can reduce confounding effects. In online panels, overrepresented populations of experienced survey-takers may respond differently than naïve participants, so mixing recruitment sources or running pilot comparisons can help detect and correct for such biases. Finally, incentives must be carefully calibrated; too high a reward can motivate participants to respond mechanically, whereas too low a reward may reduce motivation to engage fully with complex architectural stimuli. Transparent documentation of recruitment, incentive, and engagement strategies is essential for replicability and for evaluating the generalizability of findings.

Proactively exploring and gaining a deep understanding of the nuanced capabilities of each tool and methodology empower researchers to make informed, strategic decisions throughout every stage of experimental design. This deliberate engagement not only strengthens the integrity and validity of the research but also lays a solid foundation for producing meaningful and reliable findings. By explicitly acknowledging these limitations and implementing structured mitigation strategies, architects can more confidently translate survey and experimental data into actionable design insights. Recognizing the intersection between technological, logistical, and human factors ensures that experiments reflect genuine human responses to the built environment, rather than artifacts of methodological constraints.

References

Aguinis, Herman, Isabel Villamor, and Ravi S. Ramani. "MTurk research: Review and recommendations." *Journal of Management* 47, no. 4 (2021): 823–837.

Cheung, Janelle H., Deanna K. Burns, Robert R. Sinclair, and Michael Sliter. "Amazon Mechanical Turk in organizational psychology: An evaluation and practical recommendations." *Journal of Business and Psychology* 32 (2017): 347–361.

Voslinsky, Alisa, and Ofer H. Azar. "Incentives in experimental economics." *Journal of Behavioral and Experimental Economics* 93 (2021): 101706.

Chapter 13
Reporting Results: Communicating Findings Effectively

Once data collection is complete, the focus of the experimental process shifts from design and execution to analysis and interpretation. At this stage, the raw responses—each representing a participant's interaction with carefully controlled conditions—are assembled into a dataset that reflects the cumulative outcome of the study. This dataset should be clean, which substantively means removing or flagging incomplete responses, removing identifying data—as per normal IRB instructions, ensuring variable names are consistent and descriptive, and condition codes should be clearly labeled and matched to the experimental design. Time stamps, response durations, and branching logic outputs should also be reviewed to confirm that participants followed the intended path through the study. A clean dataset ensures that the analysis reflects the actual behavior and responses of engaged participants under controlled conditions, not artifacts of poor design implementation or participant error. It is the difference between conducting an analysis that tests your hypothesis and one that misrepresents it entirely.

Once the experimental data has been meticulously collected, the first and arguably most critical stage of analysis is the assessment of manipulation checks. This step is foundational because it directly addresses the internal validity of the experiment, verifying that the IV was not only successfully delivered by the experimental system but also accurately perceived and understood by the participants as intended. Without confirming the efficacy of the manipulation, any subsequent findings related to the dependent variables become ambiguous; it becomes impossible to confidently attribute observed effects to the specific architectural design or spatial condition that was varied. If participants did not perceive the difference in ceiling height, lighting quality, or material texture as intended, then any variations in their mood, comfort, or task performance cannot logically be linked back to those specific design manipulations.

Simple descriptive statistics, such as means and standard deviations, are often the initial step. For more rigorous verification, independent samples t-tests (for two conditions) or one-way ANOVAs (for three or more conditions) can be employed to

C. J. Zolan, *Best Practice for Experimental Methods in Architecture*,
https://doi.org/10.1007/978-3-032-15884-0_13

statistically confirm that the groups perceived the manipulation differently in the intended way. An acceptable pass rate for a manipulation check is generally high, often set at 80% or more of participants accurately perceiving the manipulation. However, this threshold can vary based on the subtlety of the manipulation and the established norms within the specific research area. For a very overt manipulation (e.g., a room with and without windows), a near 100% pass rate would be expected. For more nuanced changes (e.g., a slight shift in a material's reflectivity), a slightly lower, but still high, percentage might be deemed acceptable.

Upon evaluating the manipulation check results, the researcher must carefully consider what to do with participant data that fails the manipulation check. The most common and often recommended approach is to exclude the data from participants who failed the manipulation check from the primary analysis of the dependent variables. The rationale for this exclusion is rooted deeply in the principles of internal validity. If a participant did not genuinely perceive or register the intended manipulation of the architectural variable, their subsequent responses to the dependent variables are essentially noise, not true reactions to the experimental condition. Including such data would introduce uncontrolled variance, dilute any real effects, and potentially lead to erroneous conclusions, making it difficult to attribute changes in the DV to the IV.

By excluding these participants, the researcher ensures that the analysis focuses only on data from individuals who were truly exposed to and understood the manipulated variable, thereby strengthening the causal inferences drawn from the experiment. While exclusion is primary, researchers might also conduct a separate, exploratory analysis on the excluded data to understand why the manipulation failed for that subset of participants, which could inform future experimental designs or highlight specific participant characteristics. However, this secondary analysis should never replace the primary analysis based on the successfully manipulated group. The rigorous assessment and subsequent judicious handling of manipulation check failures are paramount steps that safeguard the integrity of the entire experimental study and underpin the trustworthiness of all subsequent findings.

The next stage of analysis typically involves examining the main effects of each independent variable. Main effects reveal whether a particular factor has a statistically significant impact on the dependent variable when considered in isolation, averaging across all levels of the other variables. This step is crucial because it provides a foundational understanding of whether each manipulated variable influences outcomes as hypothesized. By first establishing the presence and direction of main effects, researchers gain a clear baseline from which to interpret more complex dynamics. Main effects are typically analyzed using ANOVA or regression models, depending on the design and measurement scale of your data. In a factorial experiment, ANOVA tests whether the mean values of the dependent variable differ significantly across the levels of each independent variable, while controlling for the influence of other factors in the model. It's also important to examine effect sizes, using partial eta squared (η^2), to understand the magnitude of the effect, not just whether it's statistically detectable (Appendix F).

Interaction effects are examined after main effects because they uncover how the impact of one independent variable changes depending on the level of another. Essentially, an interaction occurs when the effect of one factor is not uniform across the conditions of a second factor. To analyze these effects, a model including both the main effects and their interaction terms is fitted simultaneously. For instance, in a two-factor experiment with factors A and B, the model estimates the individual effects of A and B as well as their combined interaction (A×B). This is important because the interaction term tests whether the influence of factor A on the dependent variable differs across the levels of factor B, or vice versa. Interpreting interactions goes beyond simply identifying statistical significance; these effects are often more complex and nuanced than main effects. When an interaction is significant, it indicates that the relationship between one independent variable and the outcome depends on the other variable's level. In such cases, conducting post hoc analyses or simple main effects tests helps clarify which specific factor combinations drive these differences.

If a significant interaction is found, simple effects analysis would explore how lighting affects occupant comfort within each type of room layout independently. This approach clarifies whether lighting has different impacts in open versus closed layouts, providing detailed insight beyond the broad interaction term. The process involves subsetting data by levels of one factor and then applying appropriate statistical tests—such as t-tests, ANOVAs, or regression analyses—within these subsets. It is important to adjust for multiple comparisons during these tests to control for inflated Type I error rates, commonly using procedures like the Benjamini–Hochberg correction (Appendix D). These tests should be carefully explained, with attention given to the interpretation of the results, being mindful of avoiding overgeneralization. Interactions often produce nuanced or sometimes counterintuitive outcomes, and it is important to interpret them in light of the research question (Murphy and Aguinis, 2022).

Checking assumptions underlying your statistical tests—such as normality, homogeneity of variances, and independence—is essential to ensure valid conclusions. If assumptions are violated, alternative methods like nonparametric tests or data transformations may be necessary. To assess normality, you can start by plotting histograms or Q-Q plots of your residuals or dependent variables to see if the data roughly follow a bell curve. Complement this with tests like the Shapiro–Wilk test for a more objective measure (Appendix G). For homogeneity of variances, Levene's test can evaluate whether different groups have similar variance (Appendix H). Independence is usually ensured through proper experimental design (e.g., random assignment), but can also be assessed by examining residual plots for patterns or autocorrelation tests if data are collected over time. If violations occur, transforming the data (e.g., log or square root transformations) or using nonparametric alternatives like the Kruskal–Wallis test can help maintain the integrity of your analysis (Appendix I).

When writing up the results of an experiment, particularly in the context of multifactor designs, it is crucial to present both the main effects and interaction effects in a way that is accessible and understandable to the reader. Main effects represent the individual influence of each independent variable on the dependent variable, while interaction effects examine how the effect of one independent variable may depend on the level of another. Experiments with multiple factors can often produce complex relationships, so it is essential to report these effects in a clear, detailed, and interpretable manner. Significant main effects should be interpreted alongside descriptive statistics and visualizations, like bar charts with error bars, to assess the practical relevance and direction of the effect.

To start, the main effects of each independent variable should be presented in a straightforward and clear manner. This means articulating how each factor, in isolation, affects the dependent variable. For example, if you are studying the effect of room lighting (bright vs. dim) and seating arrangement (single vs. group) on occupant comfort, the main effect of lighting would explain how lighting alone influences comfort, regardless of the seating arrangement, while the main effect of seating arrangement would describe how different seating choices independently impact comfort. These effects should be accompanied by relevant statistical values such as F-values and p-values, which indicate the significance of the findings. Additionally, descriptive statistics, such as means and standard deviations, should be included to provide context for interpreting the results.

Once the main effects are reported, attention must be turned to the interaction effects, which often represent the more intricate relationships between independent variables. Interaction effects are especially important when the influence of one variable on the dependent variable is modified by the presence or level of another. For example, the interaction between lighting and seating arrangement might reveal that the effect of seating arrangement on comfort is stronger when the lighting is dim compared to when it is bright. It is vital to describe these interactions clearly and visually to help the reader grasp the combined effect of the variables. Interaction plots are particularly useful for this purpose, as they allow the reader to visualize how different combinations of factors affect the dependent variable. These plots should display the means for each factor combination and clearly show any differences or overlaps in the data across conditions.

Line plots are best when factors have ordered levels (e.g., low, medium, high lighting) because they clearly show trends and how one factor's effect changes across the levels of the other. When factors are categorical without inherent order (e.g., types of materials: wood, concrete, glass), bar charts with grouped bars are often more intuitive, allowing easier comparison of means across groups. For designs with more than two factors or more complex interactions, faceted plots (small multiples) can help by breaking down interactions into separate panels for clearer interpretation. Color and shape coding can also enhance clarity but should be used judiciously to avoid visual clutter. The goal is to present the interaction so differences in slopes or patterns are immediately visible, making it easier to interpret how the combination of factors influences the dependent variable. Boxplots can also be helpful for comparing the distributions of the dependent variable across different conditions. Ensure that all figures are clearly labeled with appropriate axis titles, legends, and units of measurement, as well as informative captions that guide the reader through the visual representation of the data. Additionally, consider using error bars to represent variability and help convey the reliability of the findings.

When faced with a three-way or higher-order interaction, the sheer number of factor-level combinations (which grows exponentially) makes raw statistical coefficients incomprehensible for most audiences. Start by fixing levels of three or four factors to isolate the interaction of the remaining one or two factors. For example, in a five-factor design (A, B, C, D, E), choose fixed levels of C, D, and E (e.g., C = level1, D = level2, E = level1) and then examine the two-way interaction between A and B within those fixed conditions. Repeat this systematically across combinations of fixed levels for C, D, and E to map how the lower-order interactions vary. This reduces the complexity and highlights where meaningful interaction patterns occur. To present this clearly, generate interaction plots or heatmaps that visualize these lower-dimensional slices. For each fixed set of factors, plot how the dependent variable changes across the levels of the remaining factors. This creates a series of interpretable graphs rather than one unwieldy figure. Label these plots carefully with the fixed conditions so your audience understands the context (Fig. 13.1).

As shown above, the use of marginal means or predicted values extracted from the model for each combination helps to summarize the interaction effects. In the example, readers can quickly see how the effect of one factor depends on the other. The key insight comes from simply comparing the heights of the bars: if the differences between "Filter" and "no-filter" change depending on the type of space, you're looking at an interaction. In this case, filtering consistently improves Quality

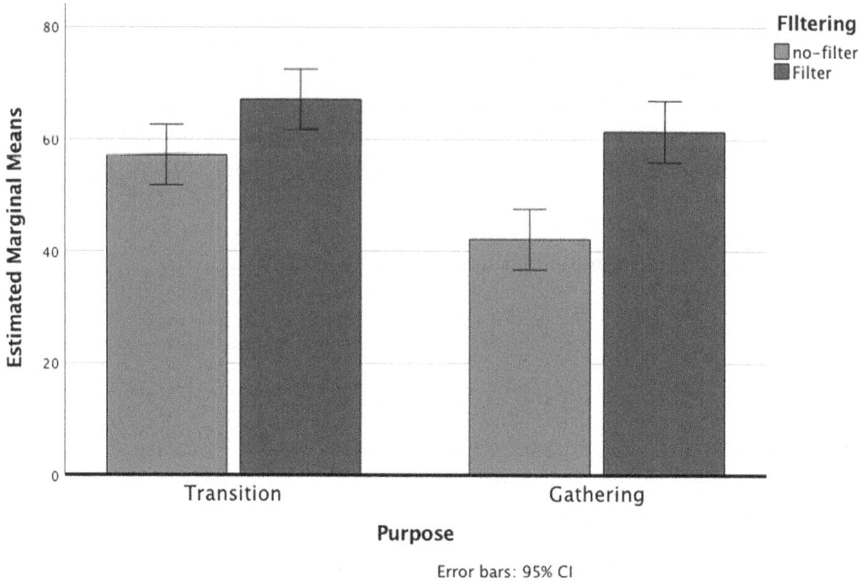

Fig. 13.1 Graph showing estimated marginal means of quality of life VAS, by presence of filtering and space use

of Life, but the size of that improvement—and where the scores start without filtering—is different for transition spaces compared to gathering spaces. The "Filter" bars are always higher, but the gap between them and the "no-filter" bars isn't the same across both space types. That shift in the pattern across conditions shows that the effect of filtering isn't uniform—it depends on the context. This kind of visual cue makes the interaction clear, even to someone without a statistics background. Reporting these estimates with confidence intervals helps quantify the magnitude and uncertainty of the interactions in an accessible way. It is crucial that the researcher fully understands complex interaction results and can explain them clearly and simply to an audience; the underlying mechanism must present a coherent rationale that makes these interactions meaningful and interpretable, because you cannot effectively communicate—or teach—findings that you yourself cannot clearly grasp.

Throughout the results section, clarity is essential. Multifactor experiments often involve complex datasets, and the results can quickly become overwhelming for the reader. To help with this, it is important to present the results in a logical, stepwise manner. Begin by presenting simpler, univariate effects before moving on to more complex interactions. It is equally important to avoid inundating the reader with too much technical detail, while still including the essential statistical information necessary to understand the findings. Figures and tables should be used to summarize key points and enhance the narrative, but the narrative itself should focus on the meaning and interpretation of the results in relation to the research question. The balance between statistical significance and practical or theoretical implications should be emphasized to show how the results contribute to the broader field of architectural research.

Finally, it is crucial to acknowledge any limitations in the results. For instance, if there are confounding factors that could have influenced the outcomes, or if certain interaction effects were weaker than expected, these should be openly discussed. Addressing unexpected or counterintuitive results in a transparent manner fosters trust in the research and provides valuable insight for future studies. By clearly presenting the main and interaction effects, using appropriate visual tools, and interpreting the findings with transparency, researchers can ensure that their experimental results are both meaningful and accessible to their audience.

Reference

Murphy, Kevin R., and Herman Aguinis. "Reporting interaction effects: Visualization, effect size, and interpretation." *Journal of Management* 48, no. 8 (2022): 2159–2166.

Chapter 14
External Validity and Other Arguments

In some humanities and social science fields, experimentalists are met with fervent disdain. In one university department, they were dubbed the "causal inference Taliban," capturing the fear of colleagues that the mere existence of experimentalists amongst them was an implicit critique of non-causal work. The approach of the non-experimentalists was to negatively perceive the work of every experimentalist—from graduate student to full professor—and dismiss it, and attempt to enforce non-experimental work while failing to try experiments themselves. In architecture, we can do better than this. Rather than letting a divide between methodological camps fuel hostility, we can recognize that experimental research and other approaches are not competitors but partners in the pursuit of understanding the built environment. After all, a few controlled experiments aren't going to ruin our ability to appreciate a well-designed building—they might just help us understand why it feels so right in the first place.

One frequent point of contention is that while experiments have robust internal validity, there are sometimes questions surrounding their external validity. External validity refers to the extent to which the results of an experiment can be generalized beyond the specific conditions and sample used in the study. This is crucial because, while an experiment may demonstrate a clear cause-and-effect relationship within a controlled environment, it is important to ask whether the same effects would be observed in real-world settings, with different populations or under different circumstances. In architecture, this issue becomes particularly relevant because environments studied in controlled experiments, such as lab spaces or simulations, may differ significantly from real buildings where factors like socio-cultural influences, diverse user needs, and contextual variables are present. While internal validity ensures that the experiment measures what it intends to measure, external validity asks whether these findings apply in broader contexts. Beyond these, experimentalists also contend with construct validity, ensuring that the theoretical concepts they intend to measure (e.g., "comfort," "privacy," "sense of well-being") or manipulate

C. J. Zolan, *Best Practice for Experimental Methods in Architecture*,
https://doi.org/10.1007/978-3-032-15884-0_14

(e.g., "spatial density," "lighting quality") are accurately operationalized and measured, reflecting the nuances of the built environment.

One of the most effective ways to strengthen the external validity of an experimental study is to sample from populations that actually reflect the users or stakeholders the research is intended to inform. While convenience samples—such as university students or anonymous online participants—are frequently used due to ease and cost, they often bear little resemblance to the intended end-users of architectural or engineering interventions. For example, a study on public housing preferences or workplace lighting should not rely solely on student participants unfamiliar with either context. By contrast, recruiting from relevant user groups—such as residents, industry professionals, or end-users of a given spatial typology—ensures that observed responses are more likely to generalize to real-world application. Architects must remember that experiments are not about producing a generic "notion of space" that applies to everyone. Instead, the focus should be on the actual users of the space under investigation. The goal is not to match national or global demographics, but to capture a representative sample of the people who will inhabit, interact with, or make decisions about the built environment. By prioritizing the lived experience and characteristics of real users, findings become actionable and meaningful for design decisions, rather than statistically impressive but practically irrelevant.

This approach may demand more logistical effort, but it aligns the sample's lived experiences, needs, and decision-making contexts with the experimental stimuli, leading to findings that are both credible and actionable.

Replication is a powerful, underused tool for increasing the external validity of experimental findings. By repeating a study across different settings, cultural contexts, or demographic subgroups, researchers can test whether an observed effect holds beyond the original conditions. This matters enormously in design-based disciplines, where spatial, social, and environmental factors vary widely across populations. For instance, an experimental finding about preference for open office layouts in a U.S. corporate context may not translate to collectivist or high-density cultures without further testing. Replication can be literal (repeating the same experiment with new samples) or conceptual (testing the same hypothesis using different stimuli or methods). Both forms help demonstrate the robustness and adaptability of the findings, and they guard against overgeneralization from a single context. In short, replication doesn't just confirm results—it extends them, providing the evidentiary foundation necessary for experimental research to inform global design practice.

It is important to acknowledge, however, that a fundamental trade-off often exists between internal and external validity. Highly controlled laboratory experiments excel at isolating causal relationships (high internal validity), but may sacrifice immediate applicability to complex real-world settings (lower external validity). Conversely, field experiments offer greater ecological relevance but may contend with more confounding variables. The experimentalist's role is not to eliminate this tension, but to strategically balance these validities based on the research question and to clearly articulate the scope and limitations of their findings. A researcher should always be prepared to demonstrate how that balance has been achieved. Pretesting and piloting can identify likely confounders and calibrate stimuli to the population of interest. Manipulation checks help verify that the experimental conditions operate as intended, even in uncontrolled settings. Stratified sampling or blocked randomization can reduce baseline differences in heterogeneous populations. Importantly, researchers should triangulate findings where feasible—either through post-experiment interviews, behavioral follow-up, or analysis of real-world correlates—to demonstrate that experimental results are both internally sound and externally meaningful. In doing so, researchers meet not only the demands of causal inference, but also the contextual depth that observational purists claim as their exclusive domain.

Experiments in architecture, like any other field, are not immune to challenges regarding external validity. For example, if a researcher tests the effect of different lighting conditions on the mood of participants in a lab, can those results be extended to how lighting in a real office or public space affects mood over time? The answer lies in careful design choices. One of the most effective tools for improving external validity is the use of random sampling from diverse, representative populations, like MTurk (McCredie and Morey, 2019). This ensures that the sample reflects the real-world diversity of users or spaces being studied, and where there is a wealth of testing to demonstrate external validity. Additionally, conducting the experiment in more naturalistic settings, such as actual buildings or environments rather than labs, enhances the external relevance of the findings. Field experiments, where conditions are manipulated in real settings, offer the opportunity to study behavior and perceptions as they naturally occur, without the artificial constraints of a controlled environment. To further bolster external validity, researchers can use replication across multiple settings and populations (Ferguson, 2004).

By repeating the experiment in different locations or with different demographic groups, one can assess whether the findings hold true across various contexts, or considering the potential moderating effects of external factors—like culture, time of day, or the specific use of space—can help ensure that the experiment's results are not overly restricted to a narrow set of conditions. In practical terms, this means architects should define the target user group carefully and recruit participants who reflect that group's demographics, behaviors, and expectations. For example, a study on a corporate office's layout should prioritize office workers with relevant experience rather than attempting to match population-wide statistics. This ensures that the insights gained are genuinely applicable to the context for which the space is being designed.

Another common critique is that experimental designs prioritize efficiency and control at the expense of ecological validity. In simpler terms, critics argue that experiments conducted in lab settings often don't reflect the messy, unpredictable nature of real-world environments. For example, an experiment conducted in a controlled room with ideal lighting and temperature conditions may not account for the variety of experiences people have in an actual architectural space that has fluctuating conditions, diverse user groups, and evolving social dynamics. The controlled nature of experiments can make it hard to generalize findings to everyday architectural practice. In response to this critique, the onus is on the experimentalist to develop experimental environments that are more ecologically valid, meaning they more closely resemble the dynamic and varied conditions of the environments they seek to understand (Holleman et al., 2020). This requires creativity and careful planning. For instance, rather than conducting an experiment in a sterile, lab-like setting, researchers might design experiments that take place in a real or semi-real architectural setting, such as a simulated office space or public area with fluctuating lighting, sound, and temperature conditions. Additionally, participants might be exposed to scenarios that replicate the complexity of actual spaces, such as group interactions, noise, or distractions, which are often present in the everyday use of architectural spaces. By developing experimental designs that better mimic the realities of architectural environments, experimentalists can mitigate criticisms of ecological validity and increase the relevance and applicability of their findings to real-world practice.

There will always be those that simply "don't trust" experiments. This skepticism often arises from the perception that experiments, by their very nature, feel neat—perhaps too neat, for some. The best response to criticism of this type is transparency in the design and analytical processes, and sometimes a polite invitation to co-author. By making the underlying assumptions and methodologies clear, experimentalists can demystify their work and open the door for others to see the value in controlled experimentation. This transparency fosters a more inclusive academic culture, where critics are invited to engage in dialogue about the limits of experimental design, while still recognizing its contributions. Instead of the experiment being seen as an exclusionary method, it can be framed as part of a collaborative approach that values rigor and precision alongside the richness of qualitative perspectives. This approach not only reassures skeptics but also helps bridge the gap between different research methodologies, allowing for a more holistic understanding of architectural phenomena that includes both quantitative and qualitative insights.

References

Ferguson, Linda. "External validity, generalizability, and knowledge utilization." *Journal of Nursing Scholarship* 36, no. 1 (2004): 16–22.

Holleman, Gijs A., Ignace TC Hooge, Chantal Kemner, and Roy S. Hessels. "The 'real-world approach'and its problems: A critique of the term ecological validity." *Frontiers in Psychology* 11 (2020): 721.

McCredie, Morgan N., and Leslie C. Morey. "Who are the Turkers? A characterization of MTurk workers using the personality assessment inventory." *Assessment* 26, no. 5 (2019): 759–766.

Chapter 15
Conclusion: The Future of Survey Experiments in Architecture

The practice of experimental research in architecture offers a powerful means of understanding the complex interactions between human behavior and the built environment. By adhering to best practices such as careful experimental design, rigorous attention to internal and external validity, and transparent reporting of results, architectural researchers can produce valuable insights that bridge theoretical understanding with tangible, real-world application. While experimental methods are sometimes met with skepticism, these challenges should not overshadow the profound potential of experimentation in advancing architectural knowledge. The key lies in the ability to create experiments that genuinely reflect the richness and complexity of real architectural contexts, ensuring that findings are both robust and eminently relevant to the diverse experiences of building occupants.

As technology advances rapidly, the possibilities for experimental research in architecture are expanding dramatically. We stand at the threshold of a design revolution, where immersive experiments within highly realistic simulated environments can capture the complexity and unpredictability of real-world spaces like never before. When paired with rigorous methodology, these tools enable architects to develop dynamic, adaptable experimental designs that reflect a broad spectrum of user experiences, yielding richer insights into how people interact with architectural environments. For too long, the discipline has relied heavily on intuition, aesthetic precedent, and anecdotal evidence to inform designs that profoundly impact human lives. While invaluable, these approaches often fall short in definitively answering why certain spaces succeed or fail in supporting well-being, productivity, or social connection.

The future of experimental design in architecture promises to expand beyond individual perception to embrace the complex dynamics of multi-person interactions within built environments. As technology advances, immersive methods like multi-user virtual reality and real-time sensor integration will enable researchers to simulate and analyze social behaviors, collaboration, and spatial negotiations in ways previously impossible. This shift recognizes that architecture is not only

C. J. Zolan, *Best Practice for Experimental Methods in Architecture*,
https://doi.org/10.1007/978-3-032-15884-0_15

experienced individually but also shaped by the collective use and interaction of its occupants. Moreover, emerging tools for tracking physiological and behavioral data at scale offer unprecedented opportunities to capture subtle, real-time responses to design variations. Coupled with advances in machine learning and data analytics, these developments will allow for richer, more nuanced insights into how spaces influence group dynamics, social cohesion, and shared well-being. Embracing these promising avenues will position experimental design at the forefront of human-centered architecture, driving innovations that respond to the complex, interconnected realities of modern living and working environments.

Experimental research provides the missing link: causal relationships between design choices and human response. It equips architects not just with ideas, but with evidence. This isn't just about academic rigor; it's about a fundamental shift towards an evidence-based practice that elevates architecture from an art form to a potent force for human flourishing. By embracing experimental methods, architects gain the power to design with unparalleled confidence, shaping environments that are not only beautiful but are rigorously proven to optimize the human experience. Commitment to empirical inquiry is what will truly define the next generation of architectural innovation, ensuring our built world serves humanity with unprecedented precision and purpose.

Appendix A: *t*-Tests

A *t*-test is a statistical test used to compare two groups and determine whether there is a significant difference between them. The idea behind the test is to figure out if the difference you observe between two groups is large enough that it probably didn't happen just by random chance. Imagine you're comparing two groups—for example, two different room ceiling heights (A = 8 ft, B = 12 ft) and how long people spend in each. The *t*-test helps you ask: "Is the difference in time spent between these two layouts large enough to be meaningful, or could it just be a random chance?"

The *t*-test looks at the difference in means (averages) between the two groups. It also considers the spread (or variation) of the data within each group. For example, if one room layout gets people to stay for 20 min on average, but the other layout gets them to stay for 30 min, the *t*-test will check if this 10-min difference is statistically significant, given the spread of times in each group. In this case, I use a two-tailed test—although the calculation is the same for a one-tailed test, because we are testing whether the difference between the two groups could go in either direction—meaning we are open to the possibility that either the higher room ceiling leads to a longer time spent, or the higher room ceiling leads to a shorter time spent. The null hypothesis in a two-tailed test would be that there is no difference in the time spent between the two rooms (i.e., the ceiling height has no effect). The alternative hypothesis would be that there is a difference, but it could be in either direction—either people spend more or less time in the higher ceiling room. When you perform the *t*-test in this setup, the *p*-value you get will reflect the probability of observing a difference as extreme as what you've found, in either direction. If the *p*-value is below your significance level (usually 0.05), you reject the null hypothesis, concluding that ceiling height does have an effect on the amount of time people stay in the room, but you don't specify which direction the effect is in until you check the means.

This test works by comparing what's called a null hypothesis with an alternative hypothesis. A null hypothesis assumes that there is no real difference between the

C. J. Zolan, *Best Practice for Experimental Methods in Architecture*,
https://doi.org/10.1007/978-3-032-15884-0

two groups (i.e., any difference is due to random chance). An alternative hypothesis suggests that there is a real difference between the groups. The *t*-test produces a *t*-statistic that tells us how big the difference is between the two groups relative to how much variation exists within each group. If the *t*-statistic is large, it suggests that the difference between the groups is meaningful. The test then calculates a *p*-value, which tells us whether the difference is statistically significant. A *p*-value <0.05 is generally considered significant. In other words, if the two groups were actually the same, we wouldn't expect to see a difference this big very often.

Let's say we have two groups of data, Group A and Group B, representing the two rooms with the only difference between the rooms being ceiling height. For example:

- Group A (Room A): 20, 22, 24, 26, 28
- Group B (Room B): 30, 32, 34, 36, 38

First, we calculate the mean (average) for each group. This is done by calculating the sum of the data values divided by the number of values in the group.

$$\text{Mean}_{\text{A}} = \frac{20+22+24+26+28}{5} = \frac{120}{5} = 24$$

$$\text{Mean}_{\text{B}} = \frac{30+32+34+36+38}{5} = \frac{170}{5} = 34$$

We then want to calculate the variance, which indicates how spread out the values are within each group. You calculate it using the following formula, which involves subtracting the mean from each value, squaring it, and summing the squared differences:

$$\text{Variance} = \frac{\Sigma\left(X_i - \text{Mean}\right)^2}{n-1}$$

where X_i represents each value in the group, the mean is the average of the group, and n is the number of data points.

$$\text{Variance}_{\text{A}} = \frac{(20-24)^2 + (22-24)^2 + (24-24)^2 + (26-24)^2 + (28-24)^2}{5-1} = \frac{40}{4} = 10$$

$$\text{Variance}_{\text{B}} = \frac{(30-34)^2 + (32-34)^2 + (34-34)^2 + (36-34)^2 + (38-34)^2}{5-1} = \frac{40}{4} = 10$$

To compare the two groups, we need to combine their variances. The pooled standard deviation (SD) combines the variability of both groups into a single estimate. The formula for the pooled standard deviation is:

$$\text{Pooled SD} = \sqrt{\frac{(n_a - 1) * \text{Variance}_A + (n_b - 1) * \text{Variance}_B}{n_a + n_b - 2}}$$

where n_a and n_b are the number of data points in each group, and the variances are from the previous step. In our case, this looks like:

$$\text{Pooled SD} = \sqrt{\frac{(5-1)*10+(5-1)*10}{5+5-2}} = \sqrt{\frac{80}{8}} \approx 3.16$$

Now that we have the means, variances, and pooled standard deviation, we can calculate the *t*-statistic. The formula is:

$$t = \frac{\text{Mean}_A - \text{Mean}_B}{\text{Pooled SD} * \sqrt{\frac{1}{n_a} + \frac{1}{b}}}$$

In the case of our ceiling height experiment, this would be:

$$t = \frac{24-34}{3.16 * \sqrt{\frac{1}{5}+\frac{1}{5}}} = \frac{-10}{3.16 * \sqrt{0.4}} = \frac{-10}{1.997} \approx -5.01$$

Once you have the *t*-statistic, you compare it to a critical value from the *t*-distribution table. The critical value depends on your chosen significance level (often 0.05) and the degrees of freedom (which is $n_a + n_b - 2$). For this example, we have 8 degrees of freedom and a significance level of 0.05, so the critical value from the *t*-distribution table is approximately 2.31 (for a two-tailed test). Since our calculated *t*-statistic is −5.01, which is far below −2.31, we reject the null hypothesis and conclude that the difference between the groups is statistically significant. This means that ceiling height has a significant effect on the time people spend in a room.

If you only expect one direction of the effect (for example, you hypothesize that higher ceilings will make people stay longer), then you could set up a one-tailed test. This would mean your null hypothesis would be that there is no difference in the time spent between the two rooms (or that the time spent is less in the higher ceiling room). In a one-tailed test, you'd only be testing whether the higher ceiling leads to more time spent, not if it could be less.

To do this, the calculation does not differ, but the interpretation of the *p*-value is different. In a one-tailed test, the critical region (where we would reject the null hypothesis) is only on one side of the distribution, either the left tail or the right tail.

If you're testing for more time spent (because you think a higher ceiling will make people stay longer), you look at the right tail. If you're testing for less time (because you think a higher ceiling will make people stay shorter), you look at the left tail. If the *t*-statistic falls in the right tail (positive difference) and the *p*-value is small enough (<0.05), then you reject the null hypothesis.

Realistically, no researcher does this by hand—but it is important to have an understanding of what the *t*-test represents, so you can identify potential mistakes. The software I recommend for use in experiments is R. It is free and uses simple coding to provide output. To perform a *t*-test on R, the code is below:

```
# Example data
layoutA <- c(20, 25, 30, 22, 28, 24)
layoutB <- c(30, 35, 40, 33, 38, 37)
# Perform a t-test
result <- t.test(layoutA, layoutB, var.equal = TRUE)
# View the results
print(result)
```

Appendix B: Chi-Square Test

A chi-square test is a statistical test used to determine if there is a significant association between two categorical variables. Essentially, it helps you answer the question: "Is there a relationship between these two variables, or could the observed relationship be due to random chance?" Imagine you're an architect studying the types of materials used in two different buildings—say Building A and Building B. You want to know if the choice of material (e.g., brick, wood, glass, etc.) is independent of the building, or if the choice of material is related to which building it was used in. A chi-square test helps you determine whether the differences you observe are meaningful or if they could have happened by random chance.

To begin with, you need to organize the data into a contingency table, which shows the frequency of each combination of categories from the two variables you're testing. In this case, you might categorize the material used (brick, wood, glass) across two buildings (A and B). In this table, the rows represent the materials, the columns represent the buildings, and the numbers represent the frequency of each material used in each building. The table would look something like this:

Material	Building A	Building B	Total
Brick	50	30	80
Wood	40	60	100
Glass	30	50	80
Total	120	140	260

Like other statistical tests, the chi-square test involves a null hypothesis and an alternative hypothesis. Null hypothesis (H_0) would state that there is no association between the building and the material choice. In other words, the materials used in Building A and Building B are independent of each other. The alternative hypothesis (H_1) sets out that there is an association between the building and the material choice. The materials used are not independent of the building they are used in.

C. J. Zolan, *Best Practice for Experimental Methods in Architecture*,
https://doi.org/10.1007/978-3-032-15884-0

Next, you calculate the expected frequencies for each cell in the table, assuming the null hypothesis is true (i.e., if the materials used in the buildings were independent). To do this, you use the formula:

$$\text{Expected Frequency} = \frac{(\text{Row Total}) * (\text{Column Total})}{\text{Grand Total}}$$

In our case, this is as follows for each cell in the table, like the below for Brick Building A:

$$\text{Expected Frequency}_{\text{Brick A}} = \frac{80 * 120}{260} \approx 36.92$$

Once you have the expected frequencies, you can calculate the chi-square statistic (x^2) using the following formula:

$$X^2 = \Sigma \frac{(O - E)^2}{E}$$

where O is the observed frequency (the actual data values in the table), E is the expected frequency (the value you calculated earlier), and the sum ($\sum$) is done over all cells in the table. For example, for the Brick, Building A cell, the chi-square contribution would be:

$$X^2 = \frac{(50 - 36.92)^2}{36.92} \approx 4.63$$

You would calculate this for all the cells and then sum them to get the total chi-square statistic. To determine the significance of the test, you also need to calculate the degrees of freedom (df). The formula for degrees of freedom in a chi-square test is:

$$\text{df} = (r - 1) * (c - 1)$$

where r is the number of rows, and c is the number of columns. In our example, there are 3 materials (rows) and 2 buildings (columns), so the degrees of freedom would be 2. Once you have the chi-square statistic and degrees of freedom, you compare the chi-square statistic to a critical value from the chi-square distribution table, based on the degrees of freedom and your chosen significance level (usually 0.05). The critical value tells you the cutoff for whether the difference is statistically significant. If the chi-square statistic is greater than the critical value, you reject the null hypothesis. If the chi-square statistic is less than or equal to the critical value, you fail to reject the null hypothesis.

Here's how you would perform a chi-square test in R:

```
# Example data (contingency table)
data <- matrix(c(50, 30, 40, 60, 30, 50), nrow = 3, byrow = TRUE)
colnames(data) <- c("Building A", "Building B")
rownames(data) <- c("Brick", "Wood", "Glass")
# Perform Chi-Square Test
result <- chisq.test(data)
# View the results
print(result)
```

Appendix C: F-Tests

F-tests are a type of statistical test used to compare the variances of two or more groups to see if they are significantly different from each other. In experimental design, F-tests are often used to assess whether the independent variables (IVs) in a study have an effect on the dependent variable (DV). They are particularly useful when you have multiple groups or conditions in your experiment and you want to know if there are overall differences between them. To put it simply, an F-test helps determine if the variation in your data is due to the factor(s) you're studying or if it might be due to random chance. For instance, in architecture, if you're comparing the effect of different lighting conditions on user comfort across multiple rooms, you might use an F-test to check if the differences in comfort ratings between rooms are statistically significant or just due to random variation.

The formula for the F-test involves two main components: the variance between the groups (mean squares between, MSB) and the variance within the groups (mean squares within, MSW). You calculate the F-statistic by dividing the variance between groups by the variance within groups:

$$F = \text{MSB} / \text{MSW}$$

Mean Squares Between (MSB) is the average of the squared differences between each group's mean and the overall mean of all groups combined. It tells you how much the group means differ from the overall mean. Mean Squared Within (MSW) measures how much the individual data points in each group differ from their respective group mean. It tells you how much variation there is within each group.

Once you calculate the F-statistic, you compare it to a value from an F-distribution table (which takes into account the number of groups and the number of data points in each group) to see if it's large enough to suggest that the differences in your data are statistically significant. If the F-statistic is greater than the critical value from the table, it means there's a significant difference between the groups. In architectural

C. J. Zolan, *Best Practice for Experimental Methods in Architecture*,
https://doi.org/10.1007/978-3-032-15884-0

research, let's say you've tested three different room layouts (A, B, and C) on user satisfaction. The *F*-test will tell you if the difference in satisfaction between the three layouts is likely due to the layout itself or just random variation among people.

One important point to note is that the *F*-test doesn't tell you which specific groups are different; it just tells you if there's an overall difference. If the *F*-test shows a significant difference, you may want to do further post hoc tests (like a Tukey's test) to figure out exactly where the differences lie between your groups.

Appendix D: Benjamini–Hochberg Procedure

The Benjamini–Hochberg procedure is a method used to control the False Discovery Rate (FDR) when performing multiple comparisons in an experiment. In simpler terms, it's a statistical technique that helps you avoid mistakenly claiming that a relationship or effect is significant when it's not—especially when you're conducting many tests at once. This is important because, in experiments where many factors or variables are being tested, the chance of finding a significant result by random chance increases. To explain this further, imagine you're running an experiment in architecture where you're comparing the effects of different room layouts on user comfort. If you run several tests (for example, comparing layout A to B, B to C, and A to C), the more tests you run, the more likely you are to find a "significant" result purely by random chance, even if there's no real difference between the layouts. The Benjamini–Hochberg procedure helps you manage this risk by adjusting the significance level for each test, keeping the overall false positive rate under control.

The procedure involves several steps, which I'll break down using a general framework:

1. *Sort the p-values.* After running your tests, you'll have a set of p-values (which measure the likelihood that the observed results are due to chance). The first step in the Benjamini–Hochberg procedure is to sort these p-values from smallest to largest.
2. *Assign ranks.* Next, you assign ranks to each p-value, starting with 1 for the smallest p-value, 2 for the second smallest, and so on. This is straightforward—just list them in order of increasing size.
3. *Calculate adjusted thresholds.* The next step is to adjust the significance level (threshold for determining if a result is "significant") for each p-value. The formula for this adjustment is:

C. J. Zolan, *Best Practice for Experimental Methods in Architecture*,
https://doi.org/10.1007/978-3-032-15884-0

$$\frac{(i)}{(m)} * Q$$

where

- i is the rank of the p-value (so for the smallest p-value, $i = 1$)
- m is the total number of tests being conducted (in our case, the number of different room layout comparisons)
- Q is the desired FDR (False Discovery Rate), often set to 0.05 or 5%

For example, if you have ten comparisons ($m = 10$) and you want to control the FDR at 0.05, the threshold for the smallest p-value will be:

$$\frac{(1)}{(10)} * 0.05 = 0.005$$

The threshold for the second smallest p-value will be:

$$\frac{(2)}{(10)} * 0.05 = 0.01$$

And so on, with each threshold increasing as the p-value ranks go higher.

4. *Compare p-values to the thresholds.* Now, compare each p-value to its adjusted threshold. If a p-value is smaller than or equal to its threshold, you consider that result to be "significant." If a p-value is larger than its threshold, you stop, and all subsequent p-values are considered non-significant.

This procedure allows you to identify true significant findings while controlling the rate of false discoveries. By adjusting the thresholds for significance, it makes the decision about whether an effect is meaningful more stringent for tests that come later in the list, which reduces the risk of falsely identifying something as significant after many comparisons.

The Benjamini–Hochberg procedure is often considered better than the traditional Bonferroni method for controlling the false discovery rate (FDR) in experiments with multiple comparisons because it offers a more balanced approach between identifying true effects and controlling for false positives. The Bonferroni correction is highly conservative, which means it reduces the risk of false positives (Type I errors) but also increases the risk of false negatives (Type II errors), meaning it may miss true effects. This is especially problematic in experiments where many comparisons are being made, because the Bonferroni method divides the alpha level (significance threshold) by the number of tests, making it more difficult for any individual test to be deemed significant. While the Bonferroni correction simply lowers the significance level uniformly for all tests, the Benjamini–Hochberg procedure adjusts the threshold based on the rank of each p-value, allowing tests with smaller p-values to maintain a higher threshold. This reduces the risk of falsely rejecting null hypotheses (finding a significant result when there is none) but also retains a higher chance of detecting real effects in the process. In architectural research, say you are comparing multiple environmental factors, such as light intensity, room temperature, seating arrangements, and ventilation, to see their effects on user comfort. Using the Benjamini–Hochberg procedure would help you avoid concluding that an insignificant difference in comfort is actually a true finding, simply because you conducted many tests. The Bonferroni method may make it very hard for any of your results to be considered significant because it applies a strict significance threshold. The Benjamini–Hochberg procedure allows for a higher chance of identifying which factors truly affect occupant comfort, without over-correcting and rejecting effects that might be real, thereby providing a more practical and informative analysis when working with multiple comparisons.

Appendix E: Tukey's HSD Procedure

Tukey's Honestly Significant Difference (HSD) procedure is a widely used post hoc test applied after an ANOVA indicates significant differences among group means. Its purpose is to determine which specific pairs of group means differ significantly while controlling the family-wise error rate, the probability of making one or more Type I errors across multiple comparisons. Unlike performing multiple independent *t*-tests, which inflate the Type I error rate, Tukey's HSD adjusts for the number of comparisons to maintain the overall significance level. The procedure compares the absolute difference between pairs of group means to a critical value called the Honestly Significant Difference. Mathematically, this critical value is computed as:

$$\mathrm{HSD} = q_{\alpha,k,df} * \sqrt{\frac{\mathrm{MS}_{\mathrm{within}}}{n}}$$

where

- $q_{\alpha,k,df}$ is the critical value obtained from the studentized range distribution corresponding to the significance level α, number of groups *k*, and degrees of freedom *df* associated with the within-group variance
- $\mathrm{MS}_{\mathrm{within}}$ is the mean square error (within-group variance) derived from the ANOVA
- *n* is the number of observations per group, assuming balanced designs

To determine if the difference between two groups *i* and *j* is statistically significant, calculate the absolute difference in their means, and compare it to the HSD value:

$$\left| \underline{X}_i - \underline{X}_j \right|$$

If this difference meets or exceeds the HSD, the null hypothesis of no difference between those groups is rejected, indicating a significant pairwise difference. Otherwise, the groups are considered statistically similar with respect to the

C. J. Zolan, *Best Practice for Experimental Methods in Architecture*,
https://doi.org/10.1007/978-3-032-15884-0

outcome variable. In practice, the Tukey HSD test is performed after fitting an ANOVA model. The within-group variance and degrees of freedom are extracted from the ANOVA summary to compute the critical q-value and the standard error of the mean difference. This approach allows for simultaneous inference across all pairs while preserving the nominal Type I error rate.

It is essential to note that Tukey's HSD assumes normally distributed residuals, homogeneity of variance, and equal or nearly equal sample sizes across groups. While the test is robust to moderate violations, severe departures from these assumptions, particularly unbalanced group sizes or heteroscedasticity, may warrant alternative methods such as the Games-Howell procedure. An excellent description of this procedure is available from Aaron Schlegel (2020).

Here's how you would perform a Tukey's HSD in R:

```
# Sample data: three groups with 10 observations each
set.seed(123) # for reproducibility
group <- factor(rep(c("A", "B", "C"), each = 10))
values <- c(rnorm(10, mean = 5, sd = 1),
            rnorm(10, mean = 7, sd = 1),
            rnorm(10, mean = 6, sd = 1))

# Perform one-way ANOVA
anova_model <- aov(values ~ group)

# View ANOVA summary to check for overall group differences
summary(anova_model)

# Perform Tukey's Honestly Significant Difference post-hoc test
tukey_result <- TukeyHSD(anova_model)

# Print the Tukey HSD test results
print(tukey_result)

# Plot the confidence intervals for the pairwise comparisons
plot(tukey_result)
```

Reference

"Games-Howell Post-Hoc Multiple Comparisons Test with Python." Aaron Schlegel's Notebook of Interesting Things, April 13, 2020. https://aaronschlegel.me/games-howell-post-hoc-multiple-comparisons-test-python.html.

Appendix F: Partial Eta Squared

Effect sizes are essential metrics that quantify the magnitude of observed effects in experimental data, providing insight beyond mere statistical significance. Partial eta squared (η^2) is commonly used in the context of ANOVA to indicate the proportion of total variability in the dependent variable attributable to a factor, partialling out variance explained by other factors. It reflects the relative importance of an effect within the model. The formula for partial eta squared is:

$$\eta^2 = \frac{SS_{\text{effect}}}{SS_{\text{effect}} + SS_{\text{error}}}$$

where

- SS_{effect} is the sum of squares for the effect of interest
- SS_{error} is the sum of squares for error (within-group variance)

Partial eta squared values range from 0 to 1, with larger values indicating a stronger effect. Partial eta squared is most appropriate for factorial designs or when examining effects of multiple independent variables simultaneously, as it accounts for variance explained by other factors in the model.

Here is how you calculate partial eta squared in R:

C. J. Zolan, *Best Practice for Experimental Methods in Architecture*,
https://doi.org/10.1007/978-3-032-15884-0

```r
# Install if needed
install.packages("effectsize")
library(effectsize)

# Fit ANOVA model
anova_model <- aov(values ~ group, data = your_data)

# Compute partial eta squared for the model
eta_squared(anova_model, partial = TRUE)
```

Appendix G: Shapiro-Wilk Test

Conceptualizing the Shapiro-Wilk Test

Imagine you draw a small hand of cards and want to know if it's come from a standard, well-shuffled deck where cards are naturally balanced. You line up your cards from lowest to highest. You then locate the middle point of all your card values. A "normal" hand should be well-balanced around that middle point, with card values spreading evenly in both directions. For example, if the middle value is 7, the low cards (2, 3) should be "balanced" by high cards (Jack, Queen). If your hand is generally symmetrical (the low cards and high cards cancel each other out around the center), the hand is deemed standard.

The Shapiro-Wilk test is a method of doing this, but with a more complicated comparison to the 'expected' order, using weighted differences instead of symmetry alone.

The Shapiro-Wilk test is a widely used statistical test that assesses whether a sample of data is drawn from a normally distributed population. Knowing whether your sample data are normally distributed is crucial because many common statistical tests—like *t*-tests, ANOVA, regression—assume normality of the data or residuals. This assumption matters because these tests rely on properties of the normal distribution to calculate accurate *p*-values and confidence intervals. If the data deviate substantially from normality, those results can become unreliable: you might get inflated Type I errors or lose statistical power to detect true effects. If your data are not normally distributed (i.e., you get a low *p*-value), it's a signal to reconsider the analysis approach. However, normality violations aren't always catastrophic. Small

C. J. Zolan, *Best Practice for Experimental Methods in Architecture*,
https://doi.org/10.1007/978-3-032-15884-0

deviations often don't materially affect results, especially in large samples, but you may use Kruskal–Wallis (Appendix I).

Normality of residuals or data is a key assumption in many parametric tests, including t-tests and ANOVA, making the Shapiro-Wilk test an important diagnostic tool in experimental data analysis. Mathematically, the test statistic W is computed by comparing the order statistics of the sample to the expected values if the data were perfectly normal. Specifically, the statistic is given by:

$$W = \frac{\left(\sum_{i=1}^{n} a_i x_{(i)}\right)^2}{\sum_{i=1}^{n} \left(x_i - \underline{x}\right)^2}$$

where

- $x_{(i)}$ are the ordered sample values
- $\underline{x}$ is the sample mean
- the coefficients a_i are constants derived from the expected values and variances of the order statistics of a standard normal distribution

A W value close to 1 indicates the data are consistent with normality, whereas smaller values suggest deviations from normality. The test produces a p-value, with a small p-value (commonly <0.05) indicating that the null hypothesis of normality should be rejected.

In R, the Shapiro-Wilk test is easily conducted using the built-in function:

```
shapiro.test(data_vector)
```

Note that the Shapiro-Wilk test becomes too sensitive in large samples. For those over 4000 observations, the test becomes extremely sensitive to even tiny departures from perfect normality. Instead, rely on Q-Q plots, histograms, or density plots. These help you see if deviations from normality are meaningful or just tiny fluctuations irrelevant to your analysis.

Appendix H: Levene's Test

Levene's test is a statistical procedure used to assess the assumption of homogeneity of variances across groups, a key prerequisite for many parametric tests such as ANOVA and *t*-tests. Ensuring equal variances among groups helps maintain the validity of these tests, as violations can increase the risk of Type I or Type II errors. Unlike some alternative tests, Levene's test is robust to deviations from normality, making it particularly suitable for experimental data that may not perfectly follow a normal distribution. The test evaluates whether the variances of the dependent variable are equal across different levels of an independent grouping variable.

Mathematically, Levene's test operates by transforming the original data into absolute deviations from the group medians (or means), then performing a one-way ANOVA on these transformed values. The test statistic is an *F*-ratio comparing the variability of these absolute deviations between groups relative to the variability within groups. The null hypothesis (H_0) of Levene's test states that the population variances are equal across groups, while the alternative hypothesis (H_A) posits that at least one group's variance differs. A significant *p*-value ($p < 0.05$) indicates rejection of the null hypothesis, suggesting heterogeneity of variances. In such cases, alternative methods like Welch's ANOVA or nonparametric tests may be more appropriate.

Here's how you would perform Levene's Test in *R*:

```
# Install the car package if needed
install.packages("car")
library(car)

# Example data frame: 'data' with outcome variable 'value' and
group variable 'group'
leveneTest(value ~ group, data = data)
```


C. J. Zolan, *Best Practice for Experimental Methods in Architecture*,
https://doi.org/10.1007/978-3-032-15884-0

Appendix I: Kruskal–Wallis Test

Conceptualizing the Kruskal-Wallis Test

Imagine you have three players, each holding a hidden hand of cards. You want to see if one player tends to have stronger cards than the others. Instead of looking at the cards themselves, you line up all the cards from everyone in order from lowest to highest, and then see how each player's cards are spread across that ranking. If one player's cards consistently land higher in the order than the others, you know that player tends to have stronger hands – it's not just luck. But if the cards are all mixed evenly, the players are probably getting equally strong hands.

In this analogy, each player is like a group in the Kruskal-Wallis test, and the ranks of the cards tell you whether the differences between groups are real or just random chance.

The Kruskal–Wallis test is a nonparametric alternative to one-way ANOVA used when the assumptions of normality or homogeneity of variances are violated, or when the data are ordinal or not measured on an interval scale. It assesses whether the distributions of a dependent variable differ across two or more independent groups. Unlike parametric tests, the Kruskal–Wallis test does not assume normality and is robust to outliers and skewed data due to its reliance on ranks, making it particularly valuable in experimental settings where these assumptions may be questionable.

This test works by ranking all observations across groups together from lowest to highest, then comparing the sums of ranks between groups. Mathematically, the Kruskal–Wallis test statistic H is calculated by:

C. J. Zolan, *Best Practice for Experimental Methods in Architecture*,
https://doi.org/10.1007/978-3-032-15884-0

$$H = \frac{12}{N(N+1)} \sum_{i=1}^{k} \frac{R_i^2}{n_i} - 3(N+1)$$

where

- N is the total number of observations
- k is the number of groups
- R_i is the sum of ranks for group i
- n_i is the sample size of group i

Under the null hypothesis (H_0) that all groups come from identical populations, the distribution of H approximates a chi-square distribution with $k-1$ degrees of freedom. A significant H statistic indicates that at least one group differs in distribution from the others, though it does not specify which groups differ; further post hoc testing is needed for pairwise comparisons.

In R, the Kruskal–Wallis test is straightforward to perform using the in-built function:

```
kruskal.test(values ~ groups)
```

given a numeric vector (values) and a grouping factor (groups).

Independence of observations remains an important assumption and is usually ensured through proper experimental design, such as random assignment. However, it can also be assessed by examining residual plots for patterns or applying autocorrelation tests if the data are collected over time. If independence is violated, data transformation or switching to other nonparametric methods might be necessary.

The manufacturer's authorised representative in the EU is Springer Nature Customer Service Centre GmbH, Europaplatz 3, 69115 Heidelberg, Germany. If you have any concerns regarding our products, please contact ProductSafety@springernature.com

Printed and bound by CPI Group (UK) Ltd, Croydon, CR0 4YY
05/10/2026
02228058-0001